HEROES OF PRO BASKETBALL

Inspiring biographical sketches of 12 men who have
made pro basketball one of today's most exciting
and action-packed sports. Beginning in the 1920s
with Nat Holman of the Original Celtics, the author
discusses the careers of George Mikan, Dolph
Schayes, Bob Cousy, Bob Pettit, Bill Russell, Elgin
Baylor, Wilt Chamberlain, Jerry West, Oscar Robertson, Willis Reed and Dave Bing.

Heroes of
Pro Basketball

by Phil Berger

Illustrated with Photographs

PRO BASKETBALL LIBRARY

RANDOM HOUSE · NEW YORK

Copyright © 1968 by Random House, Inc.
All rights reserved under International and Pan-American Copyright Conventions.
Published in the United States by Random House, Inc., New York, and simultaneously in Canada by Random House of Canada Limited, Toronto.
Library of Congress Catalog Card Number: 68-29583
Manufactured in the United States of America

To AL SILVERMAN and BERRY STAINBACK of
Sport Magazine for allowing me access to
past volumes of *Sport* while researching
this book.
To MISS MARY MITCHELL for her facility
at the typewriter. And to Cooz, the BIG O,
ELG, JERRY and the rest for making this
book possible.

Contents

Introduction

This book is about heroes of pro basketball. Since it is rare for a particular period in history to monopolize a field of endeavor, it should come as no surprise that the stars included in this volume are from both the past and present.

Although the game has changed considerably over the years, one is struck by the similarity in the qualities that make up a hero. From Nat Holman, the greatest player of the 1920s, to Dave Bing, the game's newest hero, basketball stars have arrived at their status through the old-fashioned virtues of hard work, determination and courage—though it may sound corny to some.

This is not to say that our heroes were not naturally gifted. They were. But for many of them it took great pain and effort to bring out those skills. And it may interest young readers to discover just how much these great players had to overcome.

To start with, George Mikan, Bob Pettit, Bob Cousy and Bill Russell were all cut at one time or another from their school teams. Other players, such as Oscar Robertson and Dave Bing, had to prove they were good enough even to play on their local playgrounds. And the rest—Nat Holman, Dolph Schayes, Wilt Chamberlain, Jerry West, Elgin Baylor and Willis Reed—have had to conquer assorted problems before being recognized as stars.

Choosing heroes of pro basketball is the kind of exercise that is bound to arouse differences of opinion. Space limitations have made it impossible to include all the players who qualify as legitimate heroes. Regrettably, some basketball fans may find their favorites by-passed. The 12 stars selected, with the exception of Nat Holman, have all played in the National Basketball Association. Holman played before the N.B.A. was organized. Players from the newer American Basketball Association were not considered, for the league has not yet achieved the N.B.A.'s reputation for high-caliber basketball. However, it is likely that in the near future A.B.A. players will be ranked on a par with those of the N.B.A.

PHIL BERGER

HEROES OF PRO BASKETBALL

1/Nat Holman

In the 1920s, when Nat Holman played, pro basketball was a remarkably different game from what it is today. In those days, hundreds of teams claimed to have professional status. For all it took was a set of uniforms, a place to play and a man to collect tickets. Professional leagues in the 1920s were just as tenuous and they formed and folded with seeming regularity. Considering this, it is no wonder that players had little sense of loyalty to their teams. Most of them were interested only in their paychecks. And it was not uncommon for a man to play with a particular ball club one night and with an opposing team the next.

In addition, there were few arenas with the incandescent lighting and multi-tiered seating arrangements that are in common use today. Games were more likely to be played in dim, smoky dance halls or armories, where a player risked injury every time he stepped onto the court. Often the courts were enclosed by wire netting and players would get infections from being cut by the rusty metal. In other words, the conditions under which the old-time pros played were rather shabby. The game obviously needed someone to make it respectable.

If it can be said that a single player was responsible for improving the status of pro basketball in the 1920s, that man was Nat Holman. His court skills and colorful personality put basketball in Madison Square Garden for the first time and drew unprecedented crowds in other arenas.

Holman was a slim, dark man of average height, who had perfect coordination, speed, a keen playmaking sense and superb poise. His poise was sometimes mistaken for arrogance, but that actually helped to make him a box-office attraction. For, on one hand, Holman's fans would pay to see him use his superior skills to outplay the opposition and, on the other, those who considered Holman overbearing would pay to see him humiliated.

That rarely happened, however, because Holman was too far ahead of his competitors in the game's techniques. He could run and shoot better than his opponents and was such a skilled ballhandler that teammate Joe Lapchick once said, "Nat could pass the ball to you through a keyhole."

Moreover, Holman had an immense pride in his ability, a common characteristic of today's great pro stars. For instance, there is the time he was guarding Jack Inglis, a top professional of that era. Just before the end of the game, with the score tied 28-28 (a typical score in those days), Inglis cut sharply for the basket. Holman stayed with him all the way and forced him to miss his shot. But with the ball still in play, Inglis wasn't finished. He leaped off the floor, grabbed the basket with one hand, pulled himself up, took a pass with his free hand and dropped the ball in for the winning points.

Since there was no rule at the time against such a maneuver, the referee permitted the score. But what was just as remarkable about the play was Holman's attitude toward it. "I should have been up there with him to knock away that pass," he said. Only a man with great pride could have held himself responsible for an almost unstoppable basket.

Not surprisingly, the team Holman played with during his best years (1920-28) was the greatest professional club of the era—the Original Celtics. The Celtics had obtained the game's top players through the foresight of a promoter named Jim Furey. He hired the Seventy-first Regiment Armory in Manhattan on Sunday nights and organized the Original Celtics to play solely for him. The Celtics signed contracts with him that guaranteed them salaries. These were the first individual contracts in the history of basketball.

From 1922 through 1929, in the days when a center jump was held after each basket, the Celtics played an average of 130 games a year against all comers and lost only 10 or 12. Even more remarkable was the fact that they never lost a series to any team.

The Celtics played in the best arenas in the nation—and a few of the worst, too. For in order to meet the payroll, it was often necessary to book games in small towns that had drab gymnasiums. At these times, the Celtics had to worry as much about the crowds as about the other teams.

"Oh yes, we had something called audience participation," Holman has recalled. "At a game in Scranton one night, Johnny Beckman, one of the greatest of the Original Celtics, was hit by a chunk of tobacco while he was at the foul line. Old Johnny rubbed his hand over the side of his face and hollered out, 'My God, I'm bleeding.' That was one of many funny incidents, but often we didn't know what those coal miners were going to throw at us. Many of them came to the games wearing their mining caps with carbide lamps attached and looked like pretty rough fellows."

Not all the trouble came from the *men* in the gallery. There is a classic tale of the night when Holman's huge teammate, "Horse" Haggerty, swept under the basket for a shot in a gym where the spectators sat at the very edge of the court. Suddenly Haggerty screamed, "I'm stabbed." His cry of pain and surprise was justified, for a woman in the crowd had removed the pin from her hat and had jabbed him with it.

The Original Celtics: (kneeling) Nat Holman, Davey Banks; (standing) Pete Barry, Dutch Dehnert and Joe Lapchick.

The court itself was no less hazardous. "The game was so rough we used to wear hip pads," Holman has recalled, "and many a time I went to the foul line with tears in my eyes after guys had whacked me."

And in those rugged times, players often threatened each other with physical violence. For example, one night at Madison Square Garden, a player named Willie Scrill of the Brooklyn Visitations became so enraged at being feinted out of position by Holman that he threw a punch at him. Holman ducked and the blow missed. Scrill persisted and pursued Holman the length of the court, throwing punches with both hands while Holman back-pedaled to avoid the blows. Finally, Scrill exhausted himself and had to stop the futile battle. Then Holman calmly made the foul shot that was awarded him for Scrill's behavior.

Before the 6-foot 4-inch, 220-pound Haggerty became Holman's teammate on the Celtics, he was often his opponent. In one game, Holman pretended he had been fouled by Haggerty. The referee blew his whistle and charged an infraction against the Horse. Haggerty fumed. "Don't ever do that to me again," he warned Holman, "or I'll get you." Haggerty meant what he said, for the next time Holman made believe he had been fouled, the Horse carried out his threat. He waited until the attention of the officials was focused elsewhere and then knocked Holman out cold.

Although Holman and his teammates played a

rugged brand of basketball, they occasionally displayed a flair for showmanship. "During the last four or five minutes of a game we liked to turn on the tricky stuff," Holman has said. "You know, something like the Globetrotters. People in the stands would never know which player had the ball. We played to win, but we were not above clowning it up a bit."

The clowning did not always endear the Celtics to the fans of the opposing teams, but Holman and his teammates didn't care. Conscious of their superiority and so contemptuous of all opposition that they seldom bothered to win by more than two or three points, the Celtics appeared to enjoy their notoriety—especially Holman. On one occasion, the fans tried to distract Nat by booing and jeering as he was shooting a foul, only to see the tactic backfire. To show his disdain Holman looked at the fans and, without glancing at the basket, shot the ball through the hoop. "We could make the ball talk in those days," he said, "and I was lucky to have the ball drop in. If it hadn't, they certainly would have had more reason than ever to razz me."

However, Holman had never minded razzing because, more than any of his confident teammates, he craved the attention of the crowd. As sports columnist Milton Gross has recalled: "In the days when I first came to know Holman . . . he was the greatest name in the game. I saved my dimes for weeks for a balcony seat to see the

Original Celtics play the Washington Palace Five in Madison Square Garden in 1925. I remember his arrogant stride as he came on the floor. He commanded your attention. . . . He was one of the Celtics, but he was alone."

It was true that Holman set himself apart— even from his teammates—and this factor may have helped him achieve his greatness. Columnist Gross has pointed out: "The best basketball team was not above night-owling and tom-catting. They [the Celtics] drank and they gambled and they had fun while they played, but Holman, the hub around which they moved on the floor, rarely joined them off it."

For Holman, basketball was his whole life and he didn't need other distractions. His entire day was occupied with the game. Not only was he the greatest player in pro basketball, but he also coached the City College of New York basketball team at the same time. He had come to C.C.N.Y. in 1917 as junior varsity basketball coach and varsity soccer coach. After a year in the Navy, he returned to City College in 1919 as varsity basketball coach and began the process of building the school into an eastern basketball power. In both 1923 and 1924 his teams won 12 games and lost only one and were rated with the nation's leaders.

As both coach and player, Holman was always on the move. He didn't mind this because he

loved the action. And when the two roles con-
flicted, Holman would compromise. "I would stay
with my college boys until the middle of the
game and then leave them in the hands of my assistant. Somebody would drive me to 125th Street
and I would catch the ferry. I would go into the
men's room and change into my Celtics' uniform.
We would then race across the Jersey Meadows
to some armory in Patterson and I would arrive
a couple of minutes after the game started. But
they always knew I was coming."

In the 1920s, Holman went on barnstorming
tours with the Celtics, moving night after night
to different towns and different cities. "We'd play
in an armory in Manhattan, race to Pennsylva-
nia Station with a towel on our heads, be met
there by a friend with some sandwiches, ride the
train all night, stay up talking basketball, grab
an hour's sleep in the locker room on a bench and
race off to the next game."

Although he led a frantic life, Holman was well
paid. At his peak, he drew as much as $125 for a
single game and he played as many as seven
games a week. But he was not in the game for
profit alone. Basketball was his way of life. In
fact, his whole family was just as devoted to the
sport. "There was a time way back," Holman
once recalled, "when one of my brothers, Jack,
became seriously ill and was taken to the Lenox
Hill Hospital. Naturally all of us felt duty bound
to be at the hospital. We were playing Pittsburgh

that night at the 168th Street Armory and I noticed that my family seemed to be worrying almost as much about the game as about Jack. They told me that they would hold the fort and keep me in touch with things at the hospital if I left and kept them in touch about the game."

Holman couldn't resist the offer and showed up at the armory to play that night.

Even when he coached his C.C.N.Y. team, Holman wouldn't miss the chance to join in scrimmages, a habit which once threw an opposing school into a state of profound gloom. Apparently, a scout for a team on C.C.N.Y.'s schedule slipped into the gym one afternoon and watched the team scrimmage. Predictably, Coach Holman was the best player on the floor. In fact, he was so impressive that the scout wired his boss, saying C.C.N.Y. was unbeatable because of "the greatest forward I've ever seen."

Holman retired from the pros in 1930 and, in the same year, the game rapidly lost popularity. In 1934 a reporter named Stanley Frank wrote:

> Five years ago, professional basketball ranked with baseball in organization and financial returns. But the pro game passed out of the picture . . . pictures and the radio all were blamed for the crack-up of the play-for-pay game. The influence of those factors cannot be disregarded. But I wonder how many people see a tieup between the collapse of professional basketball,

which started in 1930, and the retirement of Nat
Holman as an active player in the same year.

Even though Holman was no longer a player,
he was still a coach. From 1931 to 1934, his
C.C.N.Y. teams lost only one game a year, wind-
ing up with a three-season record of 43-3. His
1949-50 team was the only club to ever win both
the N.I.T. and N.C.A.A. titles.

Amazingly, through the years, Holman never
lost his enthusiasm for the game. Even at the age
of 60, he would often go on the floor during practice to show his players what he wanted done
and how to do it. "I never get tired of this game,"
he would say. "To me, basketball is the greatest."

2/George Mikan

Unlike most pro basketball stars, George Mikan did not spend every waking moment of his boyhood playing the game. When other youngsters in Joliet, Illinois, were practicing lay-ups and set shots in the early 1930s, George could be found sitting in the parlor of his home practicing his piano lessons.

The Mikan family believed in the importance of education, and that included piano lessons. However, George's father did not disapprove of his son's playing sports. In fact, Mr. Mikan had once played semipro baseball in Joliet and thought enough of basketball to tack a hoop on the back of the family's garage. But Mr. Mikan insisted that George pay attention to his studies, which limited the time his son could devote to athletics.

Young George wasn't a bookworm, though. When time permitted, he played baseball and basketball with his kid brother, Ed. Still, as a youngster, his earliest competitive love was not basketball but, of all things, marbles. George was such a fine marbles shooter that he won the championship of Will County when he was 10 years old. His reward was a day as honorary mayor of Joliet and a meeting with baseball's Babe Ruth in Chicago.

The rewards of Mikan's adult life, however, were not earned in marble tournaments. Mikan gained his fame and fortune by revolutionizing basketball. He did this by changing the concept of the big man's role in the game. Before Mikan came on the scene, the pivotman, or center, had been primarily a ball feeder. He would station himself in the free-throw circle and, when the ball was passed to him, feed it to players cutting toward or away from him. Only rarely did he shoot. For the pivotman was not considered a prime scoring weapon. He was simply a man who kept the ball moving about the court. And in those days the ball was moved more than it was shot, in contrast to today's run-and-shoot game. Teams generally scored 35 to 40 points a game, a total that modern professional teams usually reach before half time.

Mikan changed the cautious game of his day. He proved that a man his size (6-feet 10-inches, 240-pounds as a pro) could score. And Mikan, more than anybody else, made the pro game offense-minded, which helped the National Basketball Association to gain public acceptance.

Mikan's path to fame was not easy and he had to overcome difficulties that would have stopped most youngsters. When he first tried basketball the results were discouraging. The year he attended Joliet Catholic High School, the coach of the basketball team was delivering a pep talk when he noticed that the lumbering Mikan (then 6 feet tall) was squinting. "George," he said sadly, "I'm afraid you need glasses and I never heard of a basketball player with glasses ever amounting to anything. I'm sorry, but I'll have to cut you from the squad."

After one year at Joliet Catholic, Mikan transferred to Quigley Preparatory Seminary in Chicago to study for the priesthood. The difficulty of commuting 35 miles from Joliet to Chicago, plus a rigorous academic schedule, left him little time for basketball. When he was graduated, he decided not to enter the church but to go to DePaul University in Chicago to study law.

Until he went to DePaul, George had never been coached in basketball. "I had never played high school basketball," he has said, "although I toyed around with the game while in the line-up of the Joliet Moose team and a Chicago C.Y.O. outfit."

During his freshman year at DePaul, Mikan, now grown to 6 feet 8 inches, received very little instruction because Coach Bill Wendt was too busy with the varsity. Discouraged, Mikan thought about transferring to a school where he could get more help. He arranged to work out informally with the Notre Dame varsity, which was coached by George Keogan.

On Mikan's arrival, Keogan had him scrimmage against Notre Dame's varsity center, Ray Kuka, who proceeded to give George a memorable lesson in playing the pivot. As Mikan has recalled, "It probably was the poorest performance of my life."

Keogan was sympathetic, but he told Mikan: "George, I'm afraid basketball isn't your game. You've got a good future in your studies, keep at them." To his assistant coach, Ray Meyer, Keogan said, "He's just too awkward . . . and he wears glasses."

"I guess they just didn't think I had it," Mikan later said. "They just about broke my heart, I'll tell you that. There were a couple of days when I didn't know what I was going to do."

All that changed when DePaul got a new basketball coach for the next season—Ray Meyer. Meyer, of course, had seen Mikan's disappointing scrimmage against Ray Kuka. But the new coach could not be as fussy as Keogan had been. For DePaul usually got only the leftover players from the Chicago area after Notre Dame, Northwestern, Illinois and Loyola had finished bidding for the talent.

So Meyer set to work to see what he could do with Mikan. Every day for an hour he put Mikan through a series of special drills. He had him

George Mikan with Coach Meyer.

skip rope for at least 15 minutes to improve co-ordination between his hands and feet. He made Mikan shadowbox another 15 minutes to loosen his arm and shoulder muscles. And just when Mikan appeared to be tiring, he would order him onto the court for man-on-man speed and agility workouts against 5-foot 6-inch Billy Donato. "Billy drove him nuts for a while," Meyer has said. "It was like an elephant and a flea!"

At first, Mikan had no confidence in himself. Worried about his game, he lost 40 pounds in six weeks during his first season with Meyer. But the DePaul coach kept pushing him until Mikan was panting: "What do you want, Coach, my blood?"

The hard work showed results, though. Mikan played four years of varsity ball for Meyer and got better each year. During that time, Meyer worked to bolster Mikan not only physically but also mentally. "I had the idea," Mikan once admitted, "that officials, other players and the big crowds were against me because I was so tall. Meyer took that idea out of my head."

The coach convinced Mikan that the referees were not against him by showing game movies and pointing out every foul George had committed. "I could see," Meyer has said, "he was going to be a great basketball player if only he could stop feeling sorry for himself."

Meyer succeeded, and before long opposing players were feeling sorry for themselves. Mikan played so well on offense and defense that he

The lanky Mikan guards an L.I.U. opponent.

was selected for the All-America team three years
in a row. And in 1945 and 1946 his scoring averages were the highest of the nation's major-col-
lege players.

During the summers Mikan pitched for a baseball team in the Joliet city league and he showed

enough talent to attract the attention of a number of major league scouts. Oddly enough, he also caught the fancy of players on a state penitentiary team he pitched against. In fact, they liked him so much that they built him a special bed 8 feet long and 6 feet wide.

As a result of his prowess in both sports, Mikan received offers from baseball and basketball teams. And when he was graduated he had to decide which one to play. But he had no difficulty making up his mind, for by then basketball was in his blood.

In the 1946-47 season, Mikan made his professional debut with the Chicago American Gears in the National Basketball League, which was a rival of the Basketball Association of America. He soon found out that what he had done in college didn't impress the pros. In his very first game with the Gears, he played against "Cowboy" Edwards, who promptly knocked out four of George's teeth in vigorous infighting beneath the backboards. "They really wanted me out of that game," Mikan said, in something of an understatement.

That was indicative of what was to follow. In his first year as a pro Mikan had a great deal of trouble. In the first place, the Chicago club would not give him a long-term contract. Another point of contention was the jealousy between veteran players and Mikan, which inhibited George's effectiveness. Playing 25 games for the Gears in

1946-47, Mikan averaged only 16.5 points per game. When the Gears folded the following year, he actually felt relieved.

The Gear players were divided among teams in the National Basketball League. Mikan ended up with the brand-new Minneapolis Laker club, which had been the Detroit franchise the year before. Representing Detroit, the team had won only four of 44 games. With Mikan, however, the team won the National League title. George, happy now with his contract and teammates, scored 1,195 points in 56 games and was the unanimous choice as the league's Most Valuable Player.

The following year, the rival National Basketball Association persuaded the Lakers to shift the team into its league. Mikan and his teammates proceeded to tear the N.B.A. apart. Big George averaged 28.3 in 1948-49, his first year in the league. In the 30-day period at the close of the season, Mikan went on a scoring rampage. On Washington's Birthday, he scored 48 points against New York. Four days later, he totaled 53 points against Baltimore. He scored 51 against New York 15 days later and 46 against Rochester six days after that. But that was nothing compared to his performance against the Washington Capitols in the play-offs.

During one contest in the series, Mikan fell heavily to the floor and tried to break his fall with his right hand. His impact with the hard

Mikan leaps into the air for a lay-up in a 1953 game against the New York Knickerbockers.

boards resulted in a broken wrist. Since the play-
off money was worth between $1,000 and $1,500
per winning player, Mikan didn't intend to let the
Capitols know he was hurt.

He finished the ball game with the broken
wrist and was rushed to a hospital afterward to
have the break set in plaster. It was dawn when
Mikan finally left the hospital to catch a plane to
Minneapolis for the next game in the series.
When he arrived he told his wife, Patricia, that
his wrist was only sprained, then headed to the
Minneapolis Auditorium for the game.

Though he convinced newsmen that his wrist
was sprained, the Capitols were more doubtful.
From the start of the game, they began chopping
at his right arm, which hung almost useless at his
side. But Mikan still had his other arm and that
was good enough. Shooting only left-handed, he
managed to average 30.3 points per game for the
whole play-off series and lead the Lakers to their
first N.B.A. title.

Throughout the rest of Mikan's career, the opposition would try to stop him any way it could,
just as the Capitols had. As a result, he lost another tooth, injured his right foot, the arch of his
left foot, and broke his thumb and nose. For his
many basketball injuries, Mikan required a total
of 166 stitches during his career. Once, when
reporters asked him about an accusation made by
the New York Knicks that he used his elbows ex-
cessively, Mikan silently drew off his jersey and

with a finger traced a line of bruises running from his shoulders to his hips.

"They're complaining!" he said. "What do you think these are? Birthmarks?"

Mikan took the rough treatment without protest, for he knew it was part of the game. He considered it a breach of the player's code to allow an injury to keep him from playing. For example, one night an opposing center clawed his nose so badly that the Laker physician had to stitch the injury. But Mikan would not leave the court to have the wound attended to until he had taken the two free throws for the foul. And he made both shots.

His foes couldn't stop Mikan, but the rule makers did to a limited degree. Prior to the 1951-52 season, they expanded the foul lane from six to 12 feet and made it an automatic violation for a player on the attacking team to be in the lane more than three seconds. The purpose was to force players like Mikan away from the basket. Even though the rule reduced Mikan's 28.4 scoring average of the previous season to 23.8, the big center was still capable of scoring explosions. In a double-overtime victory over the Rochester Royals that year, he scored 61 points.

The rule may have reduced Mikan's point output, but it did nothing to alter his overall effectiveness. Led by Mikan, the Lakers continued to be the best team in the pro league, winning five N.B.A. titles in their first six years.

Big George finished his nine-year career with a total of 11,764 regular-season points for an average of 22.6 points per game, making him the first great scorer in the game. In addition, he wound up with a total of 4,167 rebounds. He was also praised for being a fine playmaker from the pivot position. Joe Lapchick, a pioneer professional with the Original Celtics, once said, "Everyone forgets that Mikan was the best feeder out of the pivot that the game ever had. If you covered him normally, he'd kill you with his scoring. If you covered him abnormally, he'd murder you with his passes."

But Mikan's contribution was more than the few lines of type that he left behind in the N.B.A. record book. His presence alone had made pro basketball a better game. His accomplishment, as writer Norman Katkov has said, "was probably summed up in the mute but magnificent tribute that always greeted the Lakers when they came to New York. There on the marquee of Madison Square Garden, the mecca of American indoor sports, it was stated in its simplest possible terms:

TONITE
GEORGE MIKAN
VS.
KNICKS

Seeing that, Mikan must have felt that all the effort—and even the blood—Ray Meyer had demanded of him was worth-while.

3/Dolph Schayes

Nobody else in the history of the N.B.A. has been quite as durable as Dolph Schayes. Other players have been slowly worn down by the frantic pace and the physical nature of the pro game, but Schayes ignored assorted bruises and broken bones to play for 16 seasons. From 1949 to 1964, he performed at forward for the Syracuse Nationals (who became the Philadelphia 76ers in 1963) with remarkable tenacity and skill.

During that time, Schayes played in a record total of 1,059 games (Bob Cousy is second with 917 games), scored 19,249 points and collected 11,256 rebounds. Six times he was named to the All-Star team and another six times he was a member of the All-Stars' second team.

But what makes Schayes's achievement particularly noteworthy is the manner in which he developed as a pro. When Dolph was graduated from New York University, the experts said that he was not tough enough for the rugged brand of ball played in the pro leagues. Although he was 6 feet 8 inches tall and weighed 220 pounds, Schayes did not appear to have either the muscle or inclination to battle the big men in the N.B.A. Even his coach at N.Y.U., Howard Cann, felt that Dolph was not cut out for professional basketball. "He's not rugged or aggressive enough," Cann said. And his criticism seemed valid.

Schayes's father had once had ambitions to be a professional prizefighter, but it seemed that none of his aggressiveness had rubbed off on young Adolph. As a youngster in the Bronx, New York, Schayes was mild-mannered and very reluctant to use his size advantage. "I was much taller than the other boys," he has said, "and very self-conscious about it. Because I didn't want to take advantage of my height with the other boys, I tried to play the game the way they did."

So instead of stationing himself near the basket, Schayes would play away from the basket and attempt longer shots.

Later, at N.Y.U., Schayes was not much more aggressive. In his first varsity game, he was so wearied by the contest that he lay flat on his back during time-outs to regain his strength. Throughout Dolph's college career, Coach Cann had to prod him to be more aggressive. At practice sessions, Cann was continually barking in rapid-fire, staccato tones, "Up Adolph! Up Adolph!" urging Schayes to battle harder for a rebound. Those words were heard so often at N.Y.U. workouts that

Dolph Schayes finds it hard to maneuver during a game against St. Louis University.

when Dolph's friends greeted him in those days, they used to say, "Up Adolph! Up Adolph!"

Although Schayes was not physically tough on the court, he was technically skilled—and with good reason. He worked very hard at it. Cann has recalled: "He was a good player at N.Y.U.—no more than that. But his mind was set on being great. He was in the gym practicing every spare minute."

In these private sessions, Schayes began to develop the two-handed set shot and assorted driving moves that were to be the basis of his offensive game as a pro. And fortunately, at N.Y.U. he was given the chance to use these skills. As Schayes once remarked: "I was lucky in one respect. Howard Cann didn't use me in the pivot. So I learned basketball in its purest form. I learned to do all the things a little man must do. When I got in with the pros, they were bigger and stronger, but I had the schooling to be able to move around them."

In his early days as a pro, it did not appear that all the schooling in the world would help Schayes survive the N.B.A. He was just too timid on the court. When other players got rough, Schayes tended to shy away from the action, encouraging further intimidation from opponents. His attitude surely would have finished his career if he hadn't altered his ways. Schayes did change, but not until Al Cervi, coach of the Syracuse Nationals, harshly criticized him for being too gentle on the court.

Cervi was an old pro basketball player himself, a tough-minded, excitable man who had never played college ball. He had emerged from a rough-and-tumble Y.M.C.A. basketball background and made himself into a top professional, despite his small size. "Al was one of the great players," Schayes has said. "Competition was Cervi's life, on and off the court. Why? I don't know. Maybe it was because he wasn't a college man and we all were and he was out to show us something. He showed it to us, all right."

In fact, Cervi showed Schayes the way to survive in the N.B.A. In the simplest and often most profane terms, he told Dolph not to permit the rough stuff the other pros were using on him. Cervi's thinking was that when a man belted Dolph with an elbow, Schayes had to retaliate with a stiffer elbow. In that way, he would earn the respect of those players who were trying to bully him.

More than that, though, Cervi taught Schayes that a player had to keep pushing himself to do better and that he could never slack off for a moment. As a pro himself, Cervi had not had great natural talent. But he had compensated for his shortcomings by all-out effort and determination. That kind of spirit soon became a part of Schayes.

Suddenly, he began to play with unaccustomed aggressiveness. When other pros resorted to physical means to stop him, Dolph would retaliate in the same fashion. In addition, he seemed to be everywhere during games, and he soon got a reputation as a man who worked diligently to improve his skills. After a while Schayes got into the habit of remaining on the court after team workouts had ended to practice on his own. Although the team's basketballs would be locked up for safekeeping, Schayes had one of his own that he would bring out from his locker. Sometimes he'd practice so long that the only way the custodians could go home was to shut off the lights in the gym and politely ask Dolph to shower.

Between seasons Schayes trained just as hard at a summer boys' camp he operated. He would finish his rigorous practice sessions by shooting 150 foul shots daily. He even devised a special way to improve the accuracy of his shooting. He had noticed that the difference between the diameter of a basketball and the inside of the hoop was about nine inches. By placing a smaller hoop within the regulation-sized one, he accustomed himself to shooting at a reduced opening and in this way sharpened his eye.

The hard work and newly acquired aggressiveness paid off for Schayes. In his rookie year he was sixth in the league in scoring, sixth in assists and one of the top rebounders. In fact, Schayes was the man on whom Syracuse came to depend.

Game after game Dolph scored, rebounded, made plays and defended. "I don't see how he does it," said George Senesky, the coach of the old Philadelphia Warriors. "If you look at his arms, you'll see a huge muscle at the biceps, but above it his arms are as skinny as a child's. That's from playing so much. By the end of the year he looks as though he's all ribs and bones."

Carl Braun of the New York Knicks has said: "What sticks in my mind about him is that every night he puts on his sneakers he plays to the best of his ability—whether it's for 18,000 here at the Garden or 800 in Syracuse. He knows only one way."

Schayes often played under the most difficult conditions, too. For example, midway through the 1951-52 season he broke a bone in his right wrist and medical authorities said he was finished for the season. But the doctors hadn't counted on Schayes's great desire to play. He missed three games because the cast the doctors had fitted him with was too heavy for playing, but then he had a special plastic cast made and was able to play once again.

The injury forced Schayes to readjust his court style, but he made the best of it. In fact, he became a better player because of his handicap. For in order to make up for the loss of scoring ability with his right hand, Schayes started to practice left-handed shooting. And eventually he became as adept at hitting with his left hand as with his right. He developed the habit of cutting across the foul line, going to the left, stopping and shooting a soft one-hander with his left hand. This tactic made him even tougher to stop.

He also improved his two-handed set shot, which already was one of his most effective scoring weapons. Since the cast prevented him from holding the ball with his whole right hand, he learned to balance and guide the ball with just his fingertips. He found this method gave him greater accuracy than he'd ever had. To the end of his career, that was the way he shot the ball.

Although the injury reduced Schayes's scoring average from the 17.0 points per game of the previous season to 13.8 in 1951-52, he managed to perform brilliantly in the crucial play-offs. In a three-game series against the Philadelphia Warriors, he averaged 20.3 and took 41 rebounds.

Then, two seasons later, Schayes broke the other wrist in a game against Boston. The injury occurred when the Celtics' Bob Harris knocked Dolph to the floor as Schayes drove to the basket. Schayes went to the locker room to receive stitches for the gash he'd suffered in the fall. When the doctor took a look at the injury, he figured that Dolph was through for the evening. But Schayes had been awarded two foul shots on the play and didn't want to quit. He urged the doctor to hurry the repair work and soon returned to the court to finish the game.

It wasn't until afterward that Schayes discovered that his left wrist had been broken. But this

time he didn't miss a single game. He remembered the gauze and special spraying material
used for hardening his plastic cast two seasons
before and had it sent to him just in time for the
next game. With the plastic cast, Schayes was
able to play effectively once again—too effectively, according to other players. "It was worth
your life to play against Dolph when he wore that
cast," an N.B.A. veteran has recalled. "When he
went in for a rebound with that arm flailing
away you had to watch out that you didn't lose a
few teeth."

Despite the injury, Schayes finished the 1953-
54 season with a 17.1 scoring average and a 12.1
rebound average. The following season he was
even better, averaging 18.8 points and 12.3 rebounds a game and leading the Syracuse club to
the championship. Not surprisingly, Dolph was the
big man for the Nationals in the play-offs, scoring
19 points per game and averaging 12.9 rebounds.

In the seasons that followed his great championship year, Schayes managed to maintain his
high standards of performance even though basketball was changing and the players coming
into the league were better and better. In 1954,
with the introduction of the rule requiring teams
to shoot the ball within 24 seconds after gaining
possession, the emphasis of the game was
changed. In Schayes's view, the rule reduced the
artistry in basketball. "The shift is away from
smartness," he said. "The twenty-four-second

With his left wrist in a cast, Schayes launches a one-hander during the 1954 play-offs.

rule doesn't give a team a chance to develop plays. It's all shooting, and the jump shot can be taken without having to maneuver an opponent so that you can work free."

The rule, however, did not hurt Schayes. He still had too much offensive equipment for defenders to stop him. His high arcing set shot, which other players called "the rainmaker," was considered old-fashioned once the jump shot became popular. But Schayes's set shot was so good that he could still score plenty of points with it.

Dolph would cock the ball at eye level and if the defender did not challenge him, he would release the shot—more often than not for a basket. But if the man guarding him chose to play him closely, Schayes had the speed and agility to drive right by him. Dolph moved so hard toward the basket that often the only way an opponent could stop him was by fouling, which frequently resulted in a three-point play—that is, a field goal plus a foul shot. Since Schayes was a deadly accurate foul shooter he was a scoring threat any time he had the ball. And, having learned to play like a small man, he had certain advantages over defenders the same size or bigger, for he was quicker and more agile.

But Schayes had more than natural skills: he had pride in his performance. He was always psychologically ready for a ball game. "The most important thing any athlete does is *get up* men-

Schayes is fouled by the Warriors' Joe Graboski during a 1957 contest.

tally before the competition starts," he would
say. "It's the difference between the ordinary,
average performance and the extra effort that
wins the game, the race, or whatever he's going
to do."

Schayes's pride caused him to set very high
standards for himself. For example, in 1957, when
he broke George Mikan's lifetime scoring record
of 11,764 points, he said, "That was a basket I
won't forget. But I wouldn't have wanted it to
come on a foul or a tip-in or anything like that.
It came just the way I hoped it would come—
on a long set shot. They stopped the game in
Philadelphia and gave me the ball."

For Schayes, part of the satisfaction of breaking the record had been the fact that he hadn't
done it the easy way. That is undoubtedly one of
the reasons why he is considered a hero of pro
basketball.

4/Bob Cousy

Not many years ago, when basketball coaches wanted to describe their hotshot guards, they might have said: "Know how good this kid of mine is? He's another Cousy, that's how good he is."

Red Auerbach, who coached the Boston Celtics and the real Cousy, would listen to that kind of talk and just shake his head in disgust. And when Auerbach happened to attend a luncheon at which a coach made the unpardonable mistake of evoking "another Cousy," Auerbach rose uninvited and said, "I'm getting awfully tired of this baloney. Every kid who can dribble a ball gets called as good as Cousy. Well, I've got news for you. There ain't nobody as good as Cooz. There never was."

In his day Bob Cousy had no equal in ball-handling and team leadership. Throughout his 13 years in the N.B.A. "the Cooz" was the most exciting player in the game. Not only did he handle the ball like a magician, but he was also a high scorer. When he retired after the 1962-63 season, he had played 917 regular season games, scored 16,955 points (an average of 18.5 points per game) and was credited with 6,949 assists.

Standing 6 feet 2 inches and weighing 180 pounds, Cousy was smaller than most players in the league. But his unusually proportioned body enabled him to do things with a basketball that taller players could never hope to do. He had sloping shoulders, a thin torso and long dangling arms. Cousy's most significant characteristics, however, were probably the great strength in his wrists and the size of his hands, which always appeared disproportionately larger than the rest of him.

"Because of his shoulders, his wrists and his hands," Auerbach once said, "Cousy can dribble from the front, either side or the back without breaking his stride, twisting his body or changing the cadence of his dribble. I've never before seen a basketball player who could do that. Everyone else has to tip off his intention somehow, usually by bending his back slightly or making a turn one way or the other."

What made Cousy great, however, was not just the way he happened to be built. His attitude toward basketball was the most important factor. Even in his last year in the N.B.A., when he was 34 years old, Cousy hustled like a rookie, prompting Auerbach to remark: "His attitude is just as it

In midair after shooting, Cousy follows the ball's flight.

always was. He came to play. He never loafs. As much as he wanted to win every year, he wants to win even more now—if that's possible. He's the captain in name and the captain in action. He sets the pace out there. He never tells me he's tired. I've got to watch him myself and pull him out when he has to be pulled."

To his teammates, he was an inspiration. Like baseball's Mickey Mantle, his presence alone seemed to add life to the team's spirit. And though he was dead-serious about basketball, Cousy had the knack of keeping the Celtics loose with his low-key humor. For instance, there is the joke that Cousy and teammate Ed Macauley once played on Auerbach. The coach had a favorite red hat that he zealously guarded from his

players, who were always threatening to steal it.
One day after practice, Auerbach went to take a
shower, leaving the hat on a chair in his view. Suddenly, while wiping soap from his eyes, he discovered the hat was gone.

"Where's my hat? Who took my hat?" he bel-
lowed.

Cousy just *happened* to be nearby when the
coach cried out.

"Don't get excited, Red," Cousy said, inno-
cently. "I know exactly where your hat is."

"I'll kill you if you did anything to it," Auerbach roared, pointing a finger at the Cooz.
"Where is it?"

"Right there," Cousy said, nodding to an ad-
joining shower.

Auerbach gasped when he saw that Macauley,
standing beneath the water, was wearing it.
When the coach rushed Macauley for the hat,
Ed threw it to Cousy who calmly cut it to shreds
with a pair of scissors. Only later, after much
shouting and threatening, did Auerbach discover
a brand-new red fedora on the front seat of his
car.

Cousy was also the team's leader in less obvious ways. He demonstrated this when Chuck
Cooper, a Negro, was denied a hotel room in
segregated Raleigh, North Carolina, where Boston was to play an exhibition game. After Cooper
made plans to leave Raleigh and travel by rail to
the team's next destination, Cousy asked Auer-

bach if he could miss curfew that night and accompany Cooper to the train station. Cousy knew that his, teammate would be lonely waiting for the train in a city that had treated him so unkindly. Auerbach agreed that it was a good idea. So Cousy, instead of sleeping, walked with Cooper through the streets of the city until four o'clock in the morning, talking of one thing and another to pass the time.

Although Cousy often boosted the team's morale in such personal ways, it was still mainly by performance that he set the standards. In 1954, for example, Cousy was hobbled with a leg injury during a game against the St. Louis Hawks. The game was close and, when Auerbach looked down the bench in Cousy's direction late in the contest, Bob indicated with a nod that he'd like to play. To Auerbach's way of thinking, an injured Cousy was better than no Cousy at all. So he proceeded to send the Cooz into the game, an act that was to make the coach look like a basketball genius. In a matter of minutes, Cousy scored two quick baskets and made a remarkable pass to Bill Sharman for the basket that won the game.

As the final buzzer sounded, Cousy limped off the court in obvious pain, even though he later told reporters that his leg wasn't really bothering him very much.

With such heroics, it was no wonder that Cousy's teammates held him in awe. "A man makes

his own shoes," said forward Tom Sanders.
"Cousy made his . . . and nobody's going to
fill them. Nobody—not ever."

Another Celtic, Frank Ramsey, said, "He's a
natural leader. I've always looked up to him."

The curious thing is that, despite all the praise,
few people thought Cousy belonged in the N.B.A.
when he came into the league during the 1950-
51 season. As writer Al Hirshberg has put it: "The
experts said that Bob Cousy . . . was too small
for the National Basketball Association. They said
he was too razzle-dazzle. They said he didn't
have the right temperament. And they said he'd
give away more points than he got because he
had such glaring defensive weaknesses."

Harsh criticism of his abilities wasn't new to
Cousy. For years, on different levels of basketball competition, he had been forced to prove he
belonged. When he was a schoolboy at Andrew
Jackson High School in St. Albans, Long Island,
he had been so unimpressive the first time he
tried out for the school team that the coach had
cut him from the squad. "Too skinny," was the
verdict.

But Cousy was determined to prove the coach
wrong. He played in a number of local leagues
that season and, wherever he performed, was
outstanding. Soon word of Cousy's ability got
back to the Jackson coach, who let it be known
that he'd be glad to take another look at the
skinny kid the next season.

Cousy got his chance for Andrew Jackson High and made good. He played well enough to win a scholarship to Holy Cross in Worcester, Massachusetts. But there he immediately ran into troubles again. Primarily, it was a matter of Cousy's razzle-dazzle style of play. He was capable of looking one way and, anticipating the whereabouts of a teammate, throwing blindly in the other direction. Usually, the teammate was exactly where Cousy had thought he would be. But the trouble was that the Holy Cross players were as surprised by the passes as the opposition. Cousy's passes often ended up skidding through their hands or off their shoulders and heads. The players felt that Cousy was making them look silly. Although that was not Cousy's intention, it was definitely the effect of his slick passes. So Holy Cross coach "Doggie" Julian had to take Bob aside and tell him to ease up on his fancy passing.

For the most part, Cousy went along with his coach—to the relief of his Holy Cross teammates. But one night he was forced to improvise, and the result was a behind-the-back dribbling maneuver that became a Cousy trademark in the pros. "I picked up that behind-the-back dribble in a game Holy Cross was playing against Loyola," he has said. "The only way I could get around a guy was by shifting the ball from one hand to the other. He had me so well guarded that I couldn't do it in front, so I did it behind my back."

As a forward for Holy Cross, Cousy leaps high to pass over his North Carolina State opponent.

Though the move was flashy, Coach Julian didn't mind since it had arisen from a game necessity. But the Crusader coach did mind when Cousy was sometimes late for practice; and he was disturbed by the independent way Bob conducted himself. To punish him, Julian occasionally would put Cousy on the bench during a game, which served only to inflame Cousy's temper.

So, even though Cousy was serious-minded about basketball, he came to the pros with the reputation of a troublemaker, which he had to live down in his early days with the Celtics. For the pros—skilled as they were—were just as unaccustomed to his passing as the Holy Cross players had been. "When fellows like Macauley and Chuck Cooper were reaching for the ball from one direction," Auerbach said, "and getting smacked with it from the other, it was obvious that something had to be done."

Auerbach did what Doggie Julian had done: he put Cousy on the bench. There, fuming, Cousy decided to change his ways. When he came off the bench he cut down on his fancy passes until the other Celtics grew accustomed to his style. Then, gradually, he began to get the ball to them in his razzle-dazzle way. He flipped it over his shoulder, passed backhand, whirled the ball behind his back or simply passed it in one direction while looking in the other. Although it was flashy basketball, Cousy didn't play that way for the sake of attracting attention. Instead, he used it to fool the opposition. "He's the trickiest ball-player I've ever seen," said Ralph Johnson of the Pistons after defending against Cousy one night. "The only time he was easy to play was when the ball was out of bounds."

The fans of opposition teams found Cousy especially frustrating. One night the Celtics were playing the St. Louis Hawks in Milwaukee and a courtside spectator began to heckle Cousy: "Cousy, you're a bum! Cousy, you're a bum!" he kept yelling as the Cooz scored basket after basket. By the end of the night the Celtic star had 34 points and the heckler was saying, "Don't that bum ever miss?"

In his rookie year, the man who wasn't supposed to belong in the N.B.A. finished ninth among scorers in the league with 1,078 points (a 15.6 average) and fourth in assists with 341. Cousy had refuted the critics in every way. For one thing, he was not too puny for the N.B.A. In fact, the rest of the league had trouble keeping up with the Cooz. If he got knocked down, he'd get up and start running again. He was also deceptively strong. "My legs," he said, "are my strongest asset. The bulk of my weight is below my waist. I look about one-sixty, but I weigh around one-eighty. Nobody ever believes that until they see me standing on the scales."

Cousy felt that his boyhood training had given him the endurance for the pro game. "I

Cousy sets up a play for his teammates.

grew up playing basketball on concrete outdoor courts on Long Island," he said. "I never played indoors as a kid. I built up my legs on those hard courts, and when it came time to play on wooden floors, it was that much easier for me."

Rather than being temperamentally unfit for the pros, as one critic had charged, the Cooz was perfect. What had been mistaken for surliness at

Holy Cross turned out to be a serious-minded dedication to the game. And, unlike many flashy players, Cousy was not greedy for points. He blended his talents with the rest of the team. And he worked hard all the time to improve himself. Even his defense, which had been poor at the beginning, improved to the point where Auerbach could say, "The Cooz doesn't embarrass himself on defense. Not any more. He's come a long way since training camp."

In his second season as a pro, Cousy was named to the All-N.B.A. team for the first of 10 straight years. The following season he started on his long reign as the league's leading playmaker. In addition to his craft as a ball feeder, Cousy was getting better as a scorer. At the end of the 1952-53 season he was third among N.B.A. scorers with a game average of 19.8, finishing just behind Philadelphia's Neil Johnston and Minneapolis' George Mikan. And that season, in a play-off game against the Syracuse Nationals, Cousy put on the greatest scoring exhibition of his career.

Up to that time, the Celtics had never won a single round in the play-off series. When they won the first game of a three-game series against Syracuse, 87-81, it seemed as if they were on their way. But with less than a minute to play in the second game, the situation didn't look as promising. The Nationals had a one-point lead and Boston had the ball. Then Cousy, who had

Cousy out-rebounds Arlen Bockhorn of the Cincinnati Royals.

scored 25 points, lost the ball and the Celtics'
chances appeared dim. To win, Syracuse had
only to hold onto the ball for the final seconds.

But the Celtics managed to steal the ball. This
time Cousy drove to the basket and was fouled.
By now, everybody in Boston Garden—players and fans—was standing. The pressure was on
Cousy. For if he missed, he would be the man
responsible for the loss. Cousy eyed the basket
and shot. The ball went in and the game went
into overtime.

Boston trailed by one point in the final seconds of the extra period. Again, Cousy was
fouled. Once more, with the outcome of the game
depending on him, the Cooz calmly sank the foul
shot. The game went into a second overtime.

This time both teams were cautious about
the shots they took. They did not shoot unless
they were sure of a basket. As the clock ticked off
the final seconds, Boston again had to make a
basket to tie the score. The ball went to Cousy.
The slender guard shot the ball and it went
through the hoop. A third overtime was needed.

By now, every Syracuse player but the five
on the court had fouled out of the game and one
of them, Paul Seymour, had sprained his ankle.
Boston was, in effect, playing against four men.
Despite that, it appeared Syracuse might win.
For with 13 seconds left in the game, the Nationals had a five-point lead. Then Cousy drove
and, as the whistle blew for a foul, the ball

dropped through the basket. After that, Cousy's foul shot cut the lead to two points. Time, however, was running out.

The Celtics stole the ball and gave it to Cousy. He dribbled across the midcourt line and, 25 feet from the basket, shot a running one-hander. The buzzer sounded while the ball was still in the air. Since Cousy had released his shot before the buzzer, it would be good if it went in. The ball spun in the air and swished through the hoop. A fourth overtime was necessary.

The pressure was tremendous, so great in fact that Boston publicity director Howie McHugh fainted in the midst of the fourth overtime. By that time, however, Boston had the lead. Cousy was hitting basket after basket and no one could stop him. Boston won, 111-105. Bob Cousy had scored 25 points in the overtime periods and 50 points in all. He would never score that many points again.

But there would be many other great moments for Cousy. After the Celtics obtained Bill Russell in the 1956-57 season, Cousy guided Boston to six N.B.A. titles in seven years before he retired. During that time, of course, coaches everywhere claimed to have a player who was "another Cousy." But as the Celtics' Tom Heinsohn said shortly before Cousy retired: "He's got so much class, I can't imagine who'll take his place."

So far, nobody has been able to do so. For there is only one Bob Cousy.

5/Bob Pettit

When Robert Lee Pettit announced his retirement from the St. Louis Hawks in 1966, Boston's Bill Russell summed up his achievements: "There's not a greater competitor in sports today than Bob Pettit. He has made 'second effort' a part of the sports vocabulary."

Russell's statement also represented the opinion held by Pettit's fellow players in the N.B.A. For Bob's persistent style of play had earned the respect of players and fans alike. In 792 regular-season games Pettit had scored 20,880 points —a remarkable average of 26.4 points per game. Ben Kerner, the owner of the Hawks, said after Pettit's retirement, "There may have been greater players, but none with greater desire and dedication."

Even as a youngster in Louisiana Pettit had been dedicated to basketball, but he had little natural ability. "I weighed 118 when I entered

Baton Rouge High," he has said, "and I was only five feet nine inches tall. At fourteen, I had more of a *figure* than a build."

With his slight physique, it is no wonder that his early athletic experiences were a series of disappointments. As a freshman at Baton Rouge, he was dropped from the school's junior-varsity basketball team after its first out-of-town game. "They took his uniform away from him, and it almost killed him," Bob's father later recalled.

However, young Pettit didn't give up. He tried other sports—though he met with little success. "In baseball I was the first kid cut from the squad," he said. "In football I got into one game for one play—as a defensive left tackle. The Catholic High School guys took one look, ran at me and the ball carrier went sixty-five yards for a touchdown."

Pettit's lack of natural ability continued to frustrate his desire to play basketball. When he went out for the school team as a sophomore, he failed again. "The basketball coach ran out of uniforms before he got to me," Pettit once said with a wry grin.

At home, Bob's parents watched him suffer. "If it means so much, let's get some lumber and nails," said his father. The elder Pettit, who was 6 feet 4 inches tall, had played a year of basketball and baseball at Westminster College in Colorado and understood his son's desire to play. So he set up a basket in the backyard. With the aid of two lights in a nearby window, young Pettit shot at the basket—sometimes as late as 9 P.M.

To encourage him, Bob's father frequently joined him in the yard to shoot baskets and advised him to skip rope and play table tennis to improve his coordination. His mother, perhaps the only person in Baton Rouge whose inaccuracy exceeded Bob's, also took a few shots every day. Looking back on it, Bob has decided that she just wanted to prove to him that there was somebody worse than he.

Despite his parents' morale-building program, Pettit's progress was slow. Although he played in a church league consisting of unskilled boys like himself, he was still unable to win any particular distinction. But he kept trying. "I would go home after games and take some old sashweights from windows and practice lifting them in front of a mirror," says Pettit. "I was about five feet eleven inches tall and you could count my ribs. I looked like a walking xylophone."

In his junior year in high school, Bob suddenly grew to 6 feet 6 inches, a height that finally gave him a place on the school team. As a starter, he averaged 14 points per game, but nobody considered him at all remarkable until his senior year.

By then Pettit was 6 feet 7 inches tall and showed definite promise. His importance to his team was demonstrated by the fact that when he was sick with the mumps Baton Rouge lost all nine of the games he missed. When he returned, Pettit helped the team win 18 straight games for the city championship, and then led it to the state title.

After graduation, Bob chose to remain in Baton Rouge and attend Louisiana State University. He felt that he was not skilled enough to compete against the more expert players he might encounter in other parts of the country. But he turned out to be better than he thought—he was a two-time All America at L.S.U., scoring 2,002 points in a three-year career.

Even as an All America, though, he wasn't sure he was good enough for the pros. After graduation from college, he seriously considered playing with a business-sponsored Amateur Athletic Union team, so he could combine business and athletic careers. Although he would make less money than he would in the N.B.A., he was attracted by the security and training offered by a business career.

In the end, however, Bob decided to try pro ball. In 1954, he signed a contract with the Hawks, who were then based in Milwaukee. (The team moved to St. Louis the following year.) At the time he entered the N.B.A., Pettit was 6 feet 9 inches tall, but he weighed only 205 pounds. He did not have an especially rugged build for the kind of ball played in the N.B.A. As a result, the pros took one look at the skinny kid and decided to give him the "business." In one

Bob Pettit winds up on the back of his neck after a rough rebound attempt.

game the Lakers' 260-pound Vern Mikkelsen shoved him so hard while jockeying for a rebound that Pettit wound up in the courtside seats. But no foul was called against Mikkelsen. Putting rookies through a rough initiation was part of the pro game.

The rough treatment at the hands of veteran players continued and it seemed that Pettit's rookie season wasn't getting off to a promising start. William "Red" Holzman, who was then coaching the Hawks, warned him: "You're getting racked up like an eight ball. I'll tell you right now—you'll never make the pros if you don't start getting rough with the big guys."

Pettit took Holzman's advice to heart and began to fight back. Soon the larger players weren't trying to bully him any more. They learned that Pettit could be rough, too.

But winning the respect of the league's bigger men was only one of Pettit's problems. "I had to learn to play basketball all over again," he has said. "In college, I played pivot, my back to the basket. It was mostly a matter of making hook shots—turning and shooting. But with the Hawks I was a forward and had to learn to drive and shoot. I had to defend and clear the backboards against men who knew their business."

Pettit learned so quickly and well that he averaged 20.4 points per game, grabbed 994 rebounds and was named N.B.A. Rookie of the Year. He also was selected for the All-Star team, an honor he earned in each of the following 10 seasons.

To the immense satisfaction of Hawks owner Ben Kerner, Pettit had become a star in his rookie year. Kerner was pleased because Pettit was one of the players he had been depending on to attract enough fans to maintain the financial stability of the team in St. Louis, the Hawks' new home.

Throughout the next 10 seasons "Big Blue," as he was nicknamed, gave the city's fans their money's worth. He could score, rebound and defend equally well. He led the N.B.A. in scoring in the 1955-56 season with a 25.7 game average and again in 1958-59 with a 29.2 average. Twice—in 1955-56 and 1958-59—he was chosen the league's Most Valuable Player. And, characteristically, he gave the team his best effort even when he was injured.

During his career, Pettit required a total of 125 stitches to close the wounds he received during games. But injuries couldn't stop Pettit. For example, while playing against the Celtics one night, he was hit across the left brow and knocked unconscious. When the doctor revived him and said that the cut would have to be sewn up, Pettit replied, "Doc, let's just delay the hospital thing until after the second half. Can't you sort of patch me up for another 24 minutes?" After receiving 14 stitches, Pettit returned to the game and scored 18 points in the last half to beat Boston.

In his third N.B.A. season, Pettit took a bad

In spite of the cast on his left wrist, Pettit fights for a rebound with the Warriors' Walt Davis.

spill on a fast break and, landing on his arm, snapped one of the bones in his left hand. Not content to remain on the sidelines, Pettit asked a doctor to make a cast for his arm so that he could play. The cast turned Pettit's hand at a strange angle, but he discovered that when he raised his arm his hand just happened to be in a perfect shooting position. Pettit soon adjusted to the cast and that season he was second in scoring (with 24.7 points per game) and rebounding (1,037). In the play-offs at the end of the season his performance was even more remarkable.

"Against Boston for the world title he was fantastic," said Kerner. "We carried the Celtics down to the seventh game before losing by two points. With an arm and a half, Bob scored two hundred and ninety-eight points in ten play-off games—almost thirty per game."

Even though Pettit had been so brilliant in his third season, he himself wasn't satisfied. He felt that he was responsible for the Hawks' failure to win the N.B.A. title. In the final seconds of the last game against the Celtics, Pettit had missed a shot that would have tied the game. For a brief moment, the ball had hung on the edge of the rim. Then it had dropped off, giving Boston the victory and title. Afterwards Pettit had said, "We fight all year for this chance, and then I have to blow the big shot at the end."

But the following season, when the Hawks faced the Celtics in a rematch for the championship, Bob did not miss very many shots. In the fourth quarter of the final game, with the Celtics ahead, 86-84, Pettit suddenly got hot. As Boston's Bill Sharman said afterward: "Pettit was a madman. He was going up in the keyhole so high that six-foot-ten Arnie Risen couldn't stay with him. In every huddle we asked each other, 'How can we stop Pettit?' "

The Celtics never found the answer. In the final quarter, Pettit scored 19 of St. Louis' last 21 points. When the Celtics threatened at the close of the game, Pettit was responsible for stopping them. St. Louis won, 110-109. Pettit scored on 19 of 34 field-goal attempts and 12 of 15 foul shots for 50 points, breaking George Mikan's play-off record for regulation championship games. Afterward, he was so exhausted that he was unable to lift his head for photographers in the locker room.

Pettit's intense effort during the game drew the praise of pros throughout the league. Said Boston's Sharman: "He's the best I ever saw at both ends of the court—Mr. Consistency. . . . He's a master of such things as going up for a shot and using one arm to fend off a guard while he pops one in. He's the best at knowing the exact time to shoot. Nobody ever went after the second or third rebound with his know-how and fight. As a fast-break starter, he's one of the hardest drivers among big men. And on top of all this he scores very high."

Pettit vies with Bill Russell for the ball during the 1957–58
play-offs against Boston.

The Lakers' Elgin Baylor said: "Outside of one-man-on-one situations, I don't compare to him. The game is mostly one of working with others, taking and giving help, and that's where Pettit is the greatest."

A simpler, but no less eloquent, tribute was muttered by the little daughter of Hawk center Chuck Share in her nightly prayers: "God bless Mommy, God bless Poppy and God bless Bob Pettit."

Despite Pettit's success on the court, however, he never allowed himself to become self-satisfied. He was always striving to improve. For example, early in his career he had taken up weight lifting. "I started lifting weights in 1956 to build my strength," he has said. "I succeeded. I used to play at 210. Later I played at 235 because of what I gained by lifting weights."

In addition to building up his strength, Pettit worked hard to time his moves on the court properly. He was not particularly fast, so he would often shoot from behind a "screen" (which consists of a player stationing himself between the shooter and the foe guarding him). This tactic gave Pettit the split second he needed to shoot his "soft-touch" jump shot. Big Blue was also an excellent rebounder. When the ball was coming off the backboard, he would pursue it with bulldog tenacity until he put it into the basket.

But the most important reason for Pettit's continued improvement was his attitude toward basketball. It never varied from what it had been when he was a determined, skinny youngster with xylophone ribs. Pettit once told writer Al Stump, ". . . as you go along in life and work hard you reach new plateaus of accomplishment. With each plateau you reach, the demands upon you become greater. And your pride increases to meet the demands. You drive yourself harder than before. You can't afford negative thinking, so you always believe you'll win. You build an image of yourself that has nothing to do with ego—but it has to be satisfied."

Perhaps that is why Bob Pettit was so great. No matter how well he played, he was never satisfied. For him the second effort was a way of life.

6/Bill Russell

In the fall of 1949, Bill Russell, a 6-foot 2-inch, 128-pound sophomore, reported to George Powles, the junior varsity basketball coach of McClymonds High School in Oakland, California. Russell, however, did not impress Powles. Not only was the boy a featherweight physically, he was awkward as well. So it must have taken Powles quite by surprise when young Russell told him he was planning to be the first All-America player to come from McClymonds.

Russell wasn't kidding, either. In those days, he had very little talent, but he was full of pride and determination. Even in junior high school, when his classmates had taunted him for his clumsiness on the basketball court and made him cry, Russell had kept working to improve. At times, it didn't seem worth the effort. As a sophomore, he was a member of the third-string junior varsity. "I wasn't really third-string," he said.

"We had 15 uniforms and 16 players, and another guy and I split the 15th uniform."

That didn't stop Russell, however. He persevered and gradually convinced even Powles that he would develop. The McClymonds coach liked the indomitable spirit of the skinny kid. He brought Bill to his home and encouraged him to keep trying, which was all Russell needed in order to play as hard as he could when he got into the "scrub" games.

As a junior at McClymonds, Russell again went out for the junior varsity. Powles had now become the varsity coach, and the new coach of the jayvees took one look at Russell and cut him after the first day of practice. "I was ready to chuck it then and there," Russell said, "but Powles told me to come out for the varsity. I sat on the varsity bench through the season, getting into games very little. . . ."

As third-string varsity center, he was merely a scapegoat for the cheering section. Toward the end of games that McClymonds led, a mocking chant of "We want Russell" would usually be heard and Powles would relent and let Bill into the game. Russell would come charging onto the court and play, as one writer has put it, "as if not only the game, but the fate of the Republic, depended on him."

His efforts generally were rewarded with more jeering, but Russell ignored that and gave it his best try. "At least," he has recalled, with a smile,

"I had my own uniform."

By the end of his junior year, Bill was 6 feet
5 inches tall and his coordination appeared to be
improving. Powles, at least, saw the potential.
He arranged a membership for Bill in a neighborhood athletic club to give the youngster more
opportunity to practice. The money for dues
came from the coach's personal funds. Russell
took advantage of the kindness and practiced
every moment he could. Once he even appeared
with a blanket and pillow and asked to be allowed
to sleep at the club and lock up after finishing his
workout. He was politely refused.

For the first time in his life, though, Russell
began to see his hard work pay off. As a senior
he was a starter, but not a star for McClymonds. Having grown to a more muscular 6
feet 6 inches, he was beginning to play the kind
of defensive game he later did in college and
the N.B.A. He blocked shots, rebounded and fed
the ball to teammates for open shots. It was an
unselfish and unspectacular style that unfortunately did not attract the interest of very many
colleges. In fact, the only college to offer Russell
a scholarship was nearby San Francisco University. But that was enough for Bill. "To me," he
has said, "San Francisco was my one chance. The
one chance I'd ever get. I was determined to make
the most of it."

Once again, though, Russell encountered those
who doubted his ability. San Francisco coach

Phil Woolpert had thought he was getting a tall player who had the classical offensive moves from the pivot. Instead, he found that S.F.U. had given a scholarship to a player who was really only a fair shooter. "Woolpert didn't think much of my ability," Russell said. "No one had ever played basketball the way I played it, or as well. They had never seen anyone block shots before."

Woolpert also had not figured on the pride that continued to drive Russell. And when Bill made his varsity debut in 1953 the coach abruptly changed his mind. That night Russell—by then 6 feet 9 inches tall and weighing 200 pounds—faced California's All-Coast center, Bob McKeen. The determined sophomore out-scored McKeen 23 points to 14, out-rebounded him and, most amazingly, blocked 13 shots, eight of them by McKeen. Shot-blocking to this extent was something that basketball people had never seen before. Traditionally, pivotmen had been broad-shouldered and overpowering players. Their strength was in scoring baskets. The tall slender pivotmen who had played before Russell were not especially quick or springy. Russell revolutionized the thinking about the role of the big man, and soon youngsters in the schoolyards were emulating the way he blocked shots. Russell was a defensive hero.

To college coaches he was more than that. In his junior year Bill dominated the game so much

Bill Russell snatches a pass well beyond the reach of La Salle's Alonzo Lewis.

that the N.C.A.A. rules committee widened the foul lane from six to 12 feet. The rule was enacted so that Russell and others like him would have to station themselves farther from the basket. Theoretically, that would make it more difficult to score.

As an S.F.U. junior, Russell had taken to directing wayward shots into the basket by leaping high into the air and tapping *downward* for the field goal. To make doubly sure that players like Russell would not have it so easy, a rule was passed forbidding them to touch the ball on its downward arc to guide in shots.

However, the changes in the rules did not have the effects envisioned. For Russell was by far the quickest of the big men and was able to time his moves and still make his tip-in shots. On defense he got better and better. Largely because of Russell and a teammate named K. C. Jones, San Francisco extended its previous season's winning streak to 56 games and won its second consecutive N.C.A.A. title. Russell, of course, was named to the All-America team, fulfilling the determined vow he had made as a gangly kid to George Powles.

The pros were next. The N.B.A. was eager to find out just how good the highly publicized Russell was—especially the Celtics. Boston had gone to a good deal of trouble to secure Russell. For years, the Celtics had been an explosive offensive team that would usually lead the league in scoring but somehow manage to finish out of first place. They had excellent players in Bob Cousy, Bill Sharman and Ed Macauley, but didn't have a big man who could get rebounds and defend against other big men. Macauley, the Celtics' center, was one of the league's top scorers, but he had always been too frail to withstand the physical contact beneath the backboards. Russell was supposed to be the man who could handle that and make Boston a winner.

To get Russell, Boston gave up Macauley and a promising rookie named Cliff Hagan to the St. Louis Hawks in exchange for St. Louis's top draft choice. Although St. Louis picked second in the draft, the Rochester Royals, who had first choice, had assured Boston president Walter Brown that they would choose Sihugo Green of Duquesne. So, in effect, the Celtics had traded for Russell. The only trouble was that the Celtics had to wait for Russell to finish playing with the U.S. Olympic basketball team in Australia.

On his return, Russell gave the Celtics a few anxious moments over the wisdom of their move. As is so often the case with college stars who come into the N.B.A., Russell was not an immediate success. First of all, he had to learn a new system of basketball. San Francisco University had played a disciplined ball-control offense, in which they attempted only those shots near the basket—and then only after they had maneuvered the ball around the court to set them up. In contrast, Coach Red Auerbach's Celtics were a fast-breaking club: when the ball came off the defensive boards, the Celtics raced downcourt and tried to take their shot before the opposition had a chance to align its defense. The Celtics' offense was less cautious than S.F.U.'s, but more explosive. By using the fast break, the Boston club could open up a commanding lead in a matter of a few minutes.

Besides the new style of offense, Russell had to adjust to the roughness beneath the backboards. The first time Bill played in New York's Madison Square Garden, the Knicks' Harry Gallatin worked him over with his hips, elbows and shoulders. He also completely outplayed Russell by moving away from the basket to obtain more room for shooting over the Celtics' center. Forced to move out when Gallatin began to hit his shots, Russell lost much of his advantage as a rebounder.

But Bill was not shattered by his reception in the pro game—he still had the pride and determination to make himself a better player. "I'm learning," he said after Gallatin had bested him. "My education will go on for some time. Until I die, I hope. When I stop learning I'll quit."

The next time Boston played New York, Gallatin again went to the outside. But this time Russell was ready and he blocked four of his opponent's shots in the first six minutes. And when Gallatin tried to get rough near the basket, Russell held his own.

Rookie Bill Russell spins around for a hook shot over the Nationals' Earl Lloyd.

But the education of Bill Russell, N.B.A. rookie, continued. A few nights later in Syracuse, the Nationals' Earl Lloyd did what Gallatin had done earlier, and more effectively, too. He moved outside and shot behind a two-man screen, and when Russell attempted to move around the screen, Lloyd simply drove the other way. Lloyd made 11 of 21 shots and gave Russell an inferiority complex.

By the end of the season, though, Russell's opponents were the ones with inferiority complexes. In one game, his shot-blocking upset Syracuse's Johnny Kerr to such an extent that Kerr had to be taken out of the game. By the end of the season, it was clear that the Celtics' move to secure Russell for their club was a stroke of genius. For the first time in basketball history, Boston won the N.B.A. title.

With Russell in the line-up, the Celtics became the greatest dynasty in the history of the N.B.A. After losing their title to St. Louis the following season, when Russell missed two games because of an injury, Boston won the championship eight straight years—a record that is unparalleled in professional team sports.

And during those great years, Russell, more than any other Celtic, was responsible for Boston's winning ways. He brought to Boston a pride in performance that affected the rest of the team. He did this the best way possible—by example. For instance, in the final game of the 1961-62 play-offs against the Los Angeles Lakers, he literally played to the point of exhaustion. With the score tied in the final seconds of regulation play, Russell leaped high to take the rebound of Frank Selvy's shot and make sure that no other Laker would tap it into the basket. Then he col-

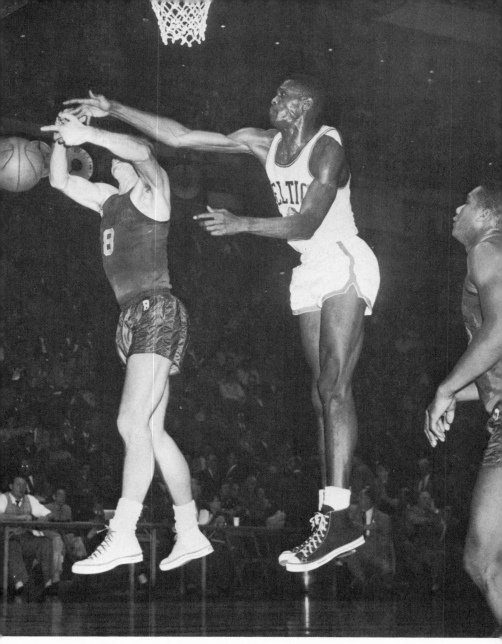

Russell blocks a shot by Bob Burrow of the Rochester
Royals.

lapsed to the floor from fatigue. Revived, he came back to lead Boston to victory by scoring four of his team's 10 points in overtime. "We like to think it's a special kind of guy who becomes a Celtic," Russell once said. "He can't be selfish and play for this team. And he's got to have pride in himself and the team."

Russell's pride often forced him to be tough on newcomers to the Celtics. In training camp, he'd test rookies with an extra shove or elbow—the way he was once tested. He did it to find out how much pride the player had, for there is no substitute for that quality. Through the years Russell's pride has enabled him to successfully battle the larger Wilt Chamberlain, who is 7 feet 1 inch tall and weighs 280 pounds.

To stop Chamberlain, Russell has had to be psychologically ready for him. Even then, there has been no guarantee that he would be able to cope with Chamberlain. For when Wilt's game is right, there is no one alive with the strength to stop him. One night, he scored 49 points against Russell and so outplayed him that the Celtic star retired to the locker room and cried. "I'm a grown man and I don't cry often, but I cried that night," Russell has recalled.

But Russell has had his nights against Chamberlain, a fact that even Wilt concedes. "Russell," said Chamberlain, "is more effective against me than any other defender in the N.B.A. because he catches me off guard with his moves. Some-

Russell and Chamberlain struggle for the ball.

times, he's playing in front to keep the ball from me. Other times, he's in back of me. He keeps me guessing. He plays me tight this time, loose the next time. I've got to look around to find out where he is. It means I'm concentrating on him as much as my shot. . . . And, of course, nobody has quite the timing he does in blocking shots."

Even after establishing himself as a pro star Russell has continued to drive himself. In the final game of the 1965-66 play-offs against the Los Angeles Lakers, Russell scored 25 points, got 32 rebounds and led Boston to a 95-93 victory and the championship. His performance was even more amazing because he shouldn't have been playing at all—he had a broken bone in his foot.

Perhaps Russell's finest moment occurred in the 1967-68 season, when, as Boston's player-coach, he rallied the Celtics and saved them from elimination in the play-offs for the Eastern Division title. Boston trailed Philadelphia, three games to one, but Russell and his teammates refused to concede and won the next two games to tie the series at three games apiece.

Then, in the final minute of the game for the Eastern crown, Russell made three big plays. In the last 34 seconds Boston led by a slim 97-95 margin, when Russell hit a foul shot to widen the lead to three points. Following a Philadelphia time-out, Bill blocked a driving shot by the 76ers' Chet Walker. And when Hal Greer missed a jump shot, Russell grabbed the rebound to keep the ball away from the 76ers in the final seconds. As the buzzer signaled Boston's victory, Russell joyously raised his fists in the air in a rare emotional gesture.

Next the Celtics met the Western Division champions, the Los Angeles Lakers, and defeated them, four games to two, for Boston's 10th N.B.A. championship. After it was all over, Russell drew the praise of the vanquished Lakers. Jerry West said, "They can talk about individual players in any sport, but I tell you that when it comes to winning there is no one like him."

Indeed Russell is worthy of such praise. The skinny kid who was taunted by his schoolmates back in Oakland has never known what it is to stop trying. And nobody could be happier about that than the Boston Celtics. Both as a player and a coach, Russell has instilled a winner's pride in the team.

7/Elgin Baylor

The first time Elgin Baylor played in the N.B.A. it took him approximately three seconds to score. As soon as the game began he took the ball, dribbled it against the floor in the stuttering fashion that is peculiar to him and then whirled toward the basket. An opposing forward, Cincinnati's Jack Twyman, moved up to defend against him and both bounded into the air at the same time. But Twyman descended first and Baylor flipped the ball into the basket. And that was how Elgin Gay Baylor introduced himself to pro basketball.

Scoring has always looked easy for Baylor, for he has the marvelous knack of seeming to hang in the air as he jumps for the basket. Sometimes, he nestles the ball at his hip, permitting his opponent to make a last desperate swipe at it, and then shoots it gently against the backboard and into the basket. Other times, he might go into the air with the defender and force his way by the man, using his thick arms and broad shoulders to protect the ball. But regardless of how he scores, he does so with a fluid grace quite remarkable for a man who is 6 feet 5 inches tall and weighs 225 pounds.

Baylor's uncanny ability to keep himself airborne prompted one newsman, Emmett Watson, to write: "He never has really broken the law of gravity, but he is awfully slow about obeying it."

At Seattle, where Baylor played his college basketball after transferring from the College of Idaho, he was so adept at maneuvering while in the air that his coach, John Castellani, remarked, "He's got more moves than a clock."

As a pro for the Los Angeles Lakers Baylor has been just as effective. His lifetime scoring average is close to 30 points per game and includes one season (1961-62) in which he averaged 38.2. In play-off games, the true test of a pro's ability to respond to pressure, Baylor has been even better. His play-off total of 3,010 points (an average of 30.7 points per game) is more than any other pro player has ever scored.

On and off the court, Baylor's style is cool. With the ball in his hands he is poised and calm. He does not grimace as some players do when concentrating on their game. He does not drive through the opposition in the mad-dash way of his teammate Jerry West. His manner is relaxed and he is not easily provoked. Referring to Baylor's calm exterior, a teammate once said: "Nor-

Elgin Baylor of Seattle University takes a rebound.

mally the big stars in this league are protected by
the refs, but not Baylor. The refs let Baylor get
pushed around more than the other big stars.
It may be that Baylor doesn't complain enough."

Actually, the Laker star doesn't think it is
necessary to complain to officials. For example,
an aggressive defender once lost his temper during a game and hit Elgin across the face. Baylor
calmly asked the player, "Have you lost your
mind?" Though he did not raise his voice, Elgin
got the message across. The warning tone in his
voice was enough to prevent further unnecessary
roughness.

Baylor's ability to remain unruffled under
stress was once dramatically demonstrated in a
snowstorm high above the Iowa plains. During
the 1959-60 season, a privately owned DC-3 air-
liner in which the Lakers were riding was taking
such a battering that the pilot was forced to radio
Iowa City for help. When he announced that he
would have to make a semicontrolled crash landing, some of the players quietly cried; others
prayed aloud. As the Lakers obeyed the pilot's
instructions to fasten their seat belts, Baylor
arose, took a blanket and moved to the rear of
the plane. He spread the blanket on the floor and
used his overcoat as a pillow. Then he stretched
out, eyes fixed on the ceiling, and said unemo-
tionally: "If I'm gonna go, boys, I'm gonna go in
style." And that's the way he stayed as the plane
landed, roughly but safely, in a farmer's field.

Despite the apparent ease with which Baylor plays basketball and handles such moments as the one just described, there have been times when he has needed more than bodily grace and a cool manner to get by. In recent personal crises Baylor's courage has been put to the test and, on these occasions, his life has been anything but easy.

Baylor's trouble started in the 1963-64 season, when his knees began to hurt. Suddenly, he was having difficulty making the moves he'd always used to get by defenders and could not score as easily as he had before. He tried bandages and heavy canvas-elastic knee braces, but they didn't appear to help. In one game against the Baltimore Bullets he found it almost impossible to make his celebrated drives and hit only three of 21 shots.

Because of his troubles, Baylor was sent to the Mayo Clinic in Rochester, Minnesota, for a checkup, but doctors were uncertain about what was plaguing him.

Meanwhile, Baylor struggled through the season with stiff knees. For the first time since the 1962 play-offs, Elgin missed a Laker game—and then he missed another. When he did play, he was not the player he had been before. By the end of the season his scoring average had dropped from the 34.0 of the previous season down to 25.4. Although most basketball fans would be satisfied with a 25.4 average, clearly

Laker fans were not. After a particularly bad game in Los Angeles, a courtside spectator roared at Baylor, "Take a vacation, bum! Do us all a favor!"

It was the first time that Elgin had ever heard such a remark from the hometown fans, and his head turned in anger to look at the man who had said it. He was hurt and would not talk about the incident with reporters. But to himself he vowed to make the fans change their opinion.

The next season Baylor's knee was inspected by the Los Angeles physician who had helped the famous Dodger pitcher, Sandy Koufax, with his arm trouble—Dr. Robert Kerlan. Earlier Baylor had learned that much of his problem stemmed from calcium deposits in his knee. This meant that small pieces of calcium, like grains of salt, were attached to the muscles in the knee and were rubbing together within the joint. Kerlan recommended pain-killing injections and exercise therapy. Although the treatment did not entirely rid Baylor of pain, it was partially effective. Baylor averaged 27.1 points per game in the 1964-65 season, but unfortunately he never got a chance to score a point in the play-offs.

Baylor's play-off series that year ended almost before it started. Early in the opening game against Baltimore, Baylor rose into the air to take a jump shot. As his feet returned to the floor, there was a popping sound and Baylor crumpled. He rose to his feet and tried to run after the play,

Baylor sits out the 1964–65 play-offs because of a badly injured knee cap.

but it was no use. He did not take more than a few steps before he collapsed to the floor again and twisted in agony. A Los Angeles crowd of 16,000 people stood in silence as Elgin was helped off the court and into the dressing room. Later, basketball fans learned that Baylor had ripped off the upper portion of his left kneecap.

Now came the hardest period in Elgin Baylor's life. After Dr. Kerlan operated on the knee, scraping free the calcium deposits at the same time, he put Baylor's left leg into a hip-to-ankle cast, and the waiting began. Baylor's chances of ever playing up to his previous standards appeared dim. "Doc Kerlan," said Elgin, "is an outspoken guy, but he didn't have much to say about my chances, and this scared me a little."

When the cast was finally removed, Baylor began the exhausting drudgery of physical therapy. He ran, pedaled bicycles and lifted weights attached to the damaged leg. For hours a day, he would strain and sweat to make his leg stronger, with no guarantee that it would be as good as it once had been. In fact, after the first few weeks of exercise his leg felt sorer and less flexible.

When the 1965-66 season began, Baylor's leg had improved, but not enough to permit him to play right away. Laker coach Fred Schaus told him to proceed at his own pace and let the Lakers know when he was ready to play. But Schaus secretly feared that Baylor might never be ready. Baylor kept working to get himself fit, but the results were not encouraging. Finally, he decided he could wait no longer to give the knee a test under game action. Dr. Kerlan agreed to the test. Baylor was given shots of pain-killing Novocain and then he jogged onto the court. However, the game did not go well for Elgin. He could not move at full speed, so Schaus was forced to use him part time.

After that, Baylor began to play more regularly, but his performances were inconsistent. One night he'd seem like the old Baylor; the next night his knee would bother him and he'd play poorly. Moreover, his knee made him vulnerable at all times to further injury.

On October 28, 1966, the Lakers were playing New York and Baylor was working extra hard

because teammate West was out with an injury.
That night he seemed to have regained the old
Baylor magic. Near the end of the first half he
had scored 19 points, grabbed 10 rebounds and
had been credited with five assists. Then, when
the half was almost over, Baylor was hurt as he
dove for a loose ball and the Knicks' Dick Van
Arsdale accidentally banged his shoulder into
Elgin's knee. Baylor winced and grabbed the
knee and Schaus and the other Lakers held their
breath.

After the game, Baylor learned that he had reinjured his knee. But that still did not stop him.
In the games that followed, Baylor played in a
state of constant pain, even though it sometimes
didn't seem worth the effort. Then in November,
Baylor strained the ligaments in his right knee. Dr.
Kerlan ordered Elgin to bed, where the right leg
was placed in another hip-to-ankle cast. Baylor
was out of action for a month, and when he returned he experienced even more difficulty than
he had with only one bad leg.

Once again, Baylor tried to make a comeback.
This time his performances were the worst of his
career. Elgin was disheartened because he knew
that his presence in the line-up was causing the
Lakers to lose ball games. But Schaus was willing
to lose a few games to give Elgin a chance to get
into shape. At first, the coach's patience appeared
to be a mistake. Baylor seemed to have lost his
skills. After a particularly bad game against De-

troit, Dr. Kerlan told him bluntly: "I can't stand watching you like this any longer. I think your knees will hold up. I don't know how much you've got left, but if you're going to come back at all, you're going to have to go all out."

Baylor nodded his head and promised to give his knees a real test and not hold back.

Kerlan's pep talk worked. Baylor's performances suddenly became better. He was forcing himself to forget about his knees and play with his customary abandon. On February 2, 1966, against Cincinnati, Baylor scored 29 points and grabbed 21 rebounds to lead the Lakers to a 119-118 victory. That night, he was moving with almost all the vigor and ease of his earlier seasons. In the locker room after the game he grinned and teased his teammates, saying, "Wasn't I a beast, baby?"

It was a beginning for Baylor, but unfortunately the season was drawing to a close. Statistically, it had been his worst year in the N.B.A. He had averaged only 16.6 and had had less than 10 rebounds a game.

But in the play-offs he gave an indication of what the league might expect from him the following season. In 14 play-off contests, he averaged 26.8 points per game and pulled down 197 rebounds.

Once again Baylor strained through the summer to be ready for the next season, pushing himself relentlessly through the exercises Dr. Kerlan

Baylor seems completely recovered from his knee injury as he shoots over the outstretched arm of the Royals' Bill Dinwiddie during a 1968 contest.

had prescribed to keep his knees strong. And when the 1966-67 season began, it was apparent that Elgin Baylor had recovered from knee injuries that had once threatened to force him into retirement. He finished with an average of 26.6 points per game. Maybe it wasn't quite as easy for him any more, but he was still one of the genuine heroes of pro basketball.

8/Wilt Chamberlain

When Wilton Norman Chamberlain was a 6-foot 11-inch, 230-pound schoolboy at Overbrook High in Philadelphia, he was considered a physical oddity rather than an athlete. "Now," Chamberlain said recently, "people have come to accept the fact that a man can be tall and talented and not be a goon. When I came along, that wasn't established and made it tough on me."

While at Overbrook, Wilt tried to prove he was no "goon." So he tended to attempt shots that would not maximize his height advantage. But no matter what he did, Chamberlain was just too good for schoolboy competition—even though opposing teams sometimes used four men to guard him.

"He's a freak," his detractors insisted. "If he weren't so tall . . ."

Chamberlain couldn't do much about his height, but he could try to show people that he was an athlete and not an accident of nature. He did this by participating in such sports as gymnastics and running, proving to some that he had all-round athletic skills. As a runner, for instance, he was good enough to hold several Amateur Athletic Union junior records in middle-distance events.

As a basketball player he was determined to improve, even though his schoolboy competition was inadequate. So Wilt often spent his time on Philadelphia playgrounds, searching for better competition. "When I was at Overbrook," he said, "I was playing in the school yards against the Golas, the Arizins, the Guy Rodgers. A man was bound to learn."

Wilt, of course, was referring to competition in a class with Tom Gola, Paul Arizin and Guy Rodgers, who all went on to join the N.B.A. The challenge of playing against such skilled boys improved his game so much that by the time he was a senior at Overbrook, he had received several scholarship offers from major basketball schools. Wilt looked forward to playing college ball because he hoped to find even stiffer competition.

Chamberlain finally selected the University of Kansas, but there he realized that nothing had really changed as far as basketball was concerned. He still scored with ease, despite double and triple-team defenses against him. And he was just as tough on defense. Iowa State's coach, Bill Strannigan, once said in reference to Wilt: "You

can't take those easy inside shots against Kansas
that you make against other clubs. You've got to
beat them from the outside."

Very few teams beat Kansas, but when they
did, it was by ganging up on Wilt. If opponents
couldn't stop Chamberlain by loading their defenses against him, they tried other methods.
In his freshman year, for instance, opposing
coaches noted that Kansas had a unique out-of-
bounds play. The Kansas player throwing the
ball back into play would lob it over the top of
the backboard. Chamberlain would leap up,
catch the ball and dunk it. Although the other
teams managed to stop the play on their own
courts by stringing chicken wire above the backboards, they didn't see how they could stop
Chamberlain on the Kansas court.

So they simply persuaded the rules committee governing college basketball to make the
whole maneuver illegal. Since stacked defenses
and what amounted to anti-Chamberlain legisla-
tion weren't Wilt's idea of competition, he soon
wearied of the college game.

Looking for other challenges, he joined the
Kansas track team after the basketball season and
won a letter as a high jumper. But this didn't
satisfy the big man, for basketball was his sport.
So, after two seasons at Kansas, Chamberlain left
school, saying: "I couldn't play basketball in any
true sense. . . . The defenses were climbing up
and down me and shoving me around like people

As a college player Chamberlain scored with ease, despite double and triple-teaming.

crowding into a subway."

Chamberlain's critics did not sympathize with him, however. They argued that, strictly speaking, Wilt was not great in any of the game's individual arts: dribbling, passing and shooting. And this time the critics were correct. But what they ignored or refused to concede was Chamberlain's uniqueness. He had height, speed, strength and agility to an extent previously unknown in basketball. And in contrast to a player like Bill Russell, Chamberlain did not have to work hard to develop his ability.

"Let's see what he does against the pros," the doubters said. "He's not going to overpower them."

While waiting to become eligible for N.B.A. basketball, Chamberlain toured the world with the Harlem Globetrotters. Wilt played at forward, which gave him a chance to develop his ball-handling skills.

Finally, Chamberlain was ready for the N.B.A. —and another round with his critics. In the 1959-60 season, playing for the Philadelphia Warriors, he began to show people just how good he could be. As early as the exhibition season, Chamberlain—having reached a height of 7 feet 1 inch and a weight of 280 pounds—was intimidating the pros. After the Celtics' Bill Russell met Chamberlain in an exhibition game, he indicated that Wilt's defensive abilities were of pro caliber and that he would be a hard man to shoot over.

"From now on," Russell said, "I retire my jump shot against Philadelphia. I'm going to put it on pension."

Once the regular season began, Chamberlain performed on the court as no other player had before him. In a contest against the New York Knicks, Philadelphia trailed by one point with only a scant 10 seconds remaining in the game. Then Chamberlain blocked a jump shot by Richie Guerin and passed the ball the length of the court to a teammate who had an opportunity for an easy lay-up. Unfortunately, the player missed his shot. But Chamberlain, after rushing downcourt, arrived just in time to take the rebound and jam it through the basket.

In another game against the Knicks, Chamberlain and New York's Kenny Sears jumped into the air simultaneously for the ball under Philadelphia's basket. Both men managed to grip the ball, but Chamberlain didn't seem to be affected. His body continued to soar upward until Sears was forced to let the ball go. At the top of his leap, Chamberlain reached above the rim and dunked the ball into the basket with both hands. It was something that only a man of overwhelming physical strength could do. And had Sears not released his hold on the ball, his hand might have been smashed against the rim as Wilt pushed the ball downward.

In a similar situation, New York's Johnny Green could not let go of the ball in time and

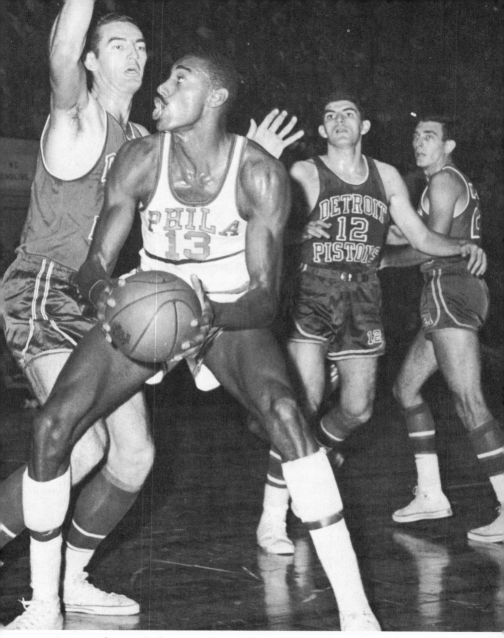

As a rookie with the Warriors, Chamberlain prepares to shoot while being guarded by the Pistons' Gary Alcorn.

Chamberlain allowed his shot to be blocked rather than injure his opponent's hand against the rim. Green admitted after the game that Chamberlain would have broken his hand had he attempted to dunk the ball.

To cope with Chamberlain, the pros at first tried to double or triple-team him, just as the opposition had done in college. But Wilt foiled the defense by passing to teammates who were free to make easy shots. Because the other Warriors sank most of these shots, opposing teams were forced to play Chamberlain one-on-one. Of course, that was the ideal situation for Wilt and, as a rookie, he set league records with his scoring average of 37.6 points per game and his total of 1,941 rebounds.

In the 1960-61 season Chamberlain was even better. He averaged 38.4 points per game and grabbed a total of 2,149 rebounds to lead the league in both departments. But even though he was by far the top offensive threat in the league, the pros were learning how to reduce his effectiveness. Syracuse's Johnny Kerr, for example, would defend against him by stationing himself to Wilt's extreme right so that the big center would be forced to turn to his left, which was his weaker shooting side. Since this also meant that Wilt ended up farther away from the basket, Kerr's strategy was a good one.

Other teams also tried to lure Wilt away from the basket by moving their big men outside on

offense and ordering them to fire away. If the
big men hit their shots, Chamberlain was forced
to leave the area near the basket and move out to
defend against the shooters, which neutralized
Wilt's height advantage.

These tactics, however, had limited success.
Chamberlain was just too good and too strong
to be stopped. Some pros even felt that he was the
greatest player in modern basketball. "He's better than any man has ever been," said Elgin Baylor. "He can run the whole game."

Bob Cousy agreed, saying: "He gets the points,
he gets the ball and he can go all night. What
else can you say?"

Other pros had opinions, too, but not all of
them were flattering to Chamberlain. "All Wilt
has going for him is his height," said Paul Seymour, then coach of the St. Louis Hawks.
"That's why I always hate to lose to him."

Even the Warriors' coach, Neil Johnston, said,
"Wilt has everything but a championship. There
will have to be changes in him and the team
before that happens."

And it wasn't long before the Warrior man-
agement followed the coach's advice: Johnston
was fired and Frank McGuire, the coach at the
University of North Carolina, was hired to re-
place him. In 1961-62, under McGuire, Chamberlain had his greatest season statistically, averaging an incredible 50.4 points per game and collecting a total of 2,052 rebounds. But once again

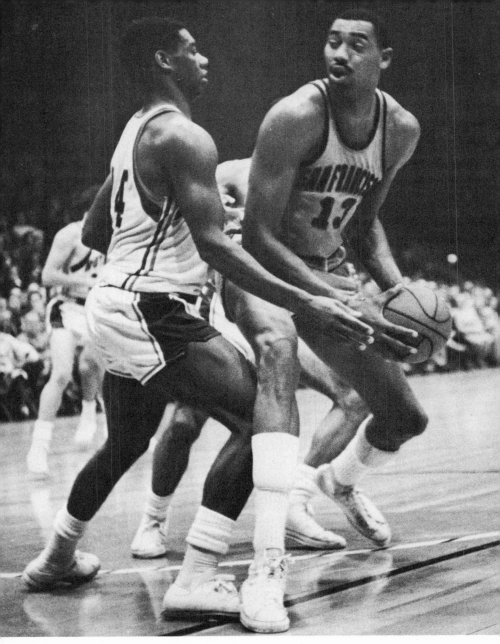

Chamberlain tries to drive past Oscar Robertson.

the Warriors lost both the Eastern Division championship and the play-offs to the Celtics.

The fact that Chamberlain could average more than 50 points a game and still not lead the Warriors to a championship seemed to be a convincing argument that he was more interested in personal glory than team play. And for the next five years—while Chamberlain moved from Philadelphia to San Francisco with the Warriors and back to Philadelphia to join the 76ers—people would say that he was not a winning ballplayer. Although Wilt finished each season with better statistics than the Celtics' Bill Russell, most basketball experts felt that Russell, the team player, was more valuable.

Not surprisingly, Chamberlain had a different viewpoint on the matter: "If I was playing for Boston, maybe I'd play like Russell," Wilt said. "If Russell played for Philadelphia, maybe he'd score more. With Boston he doesn't have to score a point. Look at that talent around him— the best in the league."

In 1965-66 the championship talent that Chamberlain was referring to appeared to be present on the Philadelphia team. The 76ers had the most powerful group of cornermen in the league. Chet Walker was one forward; Luke Jackson alternated with Billy Cunningham as the other; and burly Dave Gambee was the relief man. The backcourt was composed of Wally Jones and Hal Greer, who were fast men and good scorers. For

Chamberlain shoots a fade-away one-hander as Bill Russell attempts to block the shot.

once, Chamberlain had all the help he needed and that season the Philadelphia 76ers defeated Boston for the Eastern Division title.

However, in the play-offs, Philadelphia seemed to crumble under the pressure, losing four of five games to the Celtics, who won their eighth straight N.B.A. title.

The following season the 76ers had a new coach named Alex Hannum. Hannum had coached Chamberlain at San Francisco, where he had persuaded Wilt to pass the ball more often and sacrifice his own scoring totals for the benefit of the team. So it was not surprising that, when Hannum became coach of the 76ers, Chamberlain again responded dramatically to his advice to pass the ball.

Soon the Philadelphia attack became the most potent in the league. Though Wilt's scoring average in 1966-67 was only 24.1 points per game, the lowest of his career, he was credited with 630 assists, a career high and the third-best that season in the N.B.A.

Largely as a result of Chamberlain's unselfish ball handling, Philadelphia won the Eastern Division title with a record of 68 victories and 13 defeats, the best in the history of the league. And Wilt was an overwhelming choice for the Most Valuable Player.

Despite the honor, there still remained the job of refuting the critics' contention that he was a "loser," which meant that Wilt had to lead the 76ers through the play-offs to the team's first championship. Even though Philadelphia had been superior to the rest of the league during regular-season play, Chamberlain and his teammates knew that their record was no guarantee of success in the play-offs. For the previous season Philadelphia had been in the same position and had been humiliated by Boston. The 76ers vowed to win this time.

From the start of the play-offs, Chamberlain showed that he was serious about winning. In the semifinal Eastern series against Cincinnati, he tied a play-off record and was credited with 19 assists. On the same night he also collected 30 rebounds, blocked 12 shots and scored 16 points. In another game, when the Cincinnati defenders guarded the other 76ers tightly, Wilt did most of the shooting and scored 58 points, hitting 26 of 34 shots from the floor. Philadelphia took three of four games from Cincinnati.

Next the 76ers met Boston in the Eastern finals. Chamberlain obviously had not forgotten that the Celtics were responsible for his reputation as a loser. He produced one of the greatest performances of his career. In the important third game of the series he set a play-off record by grabbing 41 rebounds. Philadelphia won, 115-104, and ended up taking the series, four games to one.

The 76ers then went on to defeat the San Francisco Warriors for the N.B.A. championship. In

Chamberlain forces Boston's Larry Siegfried to pass off during the 1966–67 play-offs.

15 play-off contests, Wilt averaged 21.7 points per game and finished with a total of 437 rebounds and 135 assists. It was a record he could be proud of. But more important to him was the fact that he had silenced his critics on the most important count—he was at last a winner.

9/Jerry West

When Jerry West was 10 years old, he nearly drove his mother to distraction with basketball. In those days, he played on a makeshift court in a neighbor's backyard in his hometown of Cheylan, West Virginia. The cheap metal hoop, nailed on a backboard, rattled each time the ball hit it; both the hoop and the backboard were attached to the rear of a garage. Although the court wasn't fancy, young West loved it. His mother? . . . Sometimes she wondered about her boy.

Every day, when he came home from school, Jerry would grab his ball with scarcely a word and go out to practice on that backyard court. He would stay there until it grew dark—in good weather and bad—occasionally to the annoyance of his mother.

"We've always been the type of folks who believe that counseling is as good as the rod or the switch," said Mrs. West. "But one day . . . heavens! Jerry came in out of the rain three times to change his muddy shoes. The fourth time was just once too much. I bent him over my knee and gave him a good paddling."

But it didn't stop Jerry, who eventually grew old enough to go to the University of West Virginia, where he continued to play basketball. He played well enough to be an All America for three straight years and, quite naturally, he became something of a celebrity. While at the University, he received an invitation to visit the governor of West Virginia, an invitation that he was pleased to accept. When he arrived at the governor's office, he told the receptionist: "I'm Jerry West. I have an appointment with the governor." The receptionist smiled and responded: "You don't have to tell me who you are. You're better known than the governor."

Despite all the attention he received as a college star, Jerry never became blasé about basketball. In his junior year at West Virginia, he gave up his Easter vacation to play in post-season games. And when a reporter asked West's college coach, Fred Schaus (who later coached him in the N.B.A.), if he thought that playing so many games would make Jerry lose his desire for basketball, Schaus said, "Look at him, does he seem tired of it?"

Indeed he didn't. At that very moment West was sitting nervously on the sidelines, presumably to take a breather during a team practice. But West couldn't sit still—at least not on a basketball

Jerry West in action at the University of West Virginia.

court. While the players were running toward
one basket, he scooped up an extra ball, dribbled
onto the court and took two quick shots at the
other basket. He just couldn't keep away from
the action.

Since graduating from West Virginia, he has played professional basketball for the Los Angeles Lakers—and with considerable success. Each season, West averages his customary 27 or 28 points a game, is named to the N.B.A.'s All-Star team and becomes a bit more of a basketball legend. Despite his fame and a handsome salary, West is still crazy about the game. During his pro career, there have been times when Laker coach Fred Schaus and his successor, Bill van Breda Kolff, have had to take the ball from him after practice and tell him, with a patient smile, that it might be a good idea to get on home.

"I know I love basketball as much now as I did ten years ago," Jerry said recently, "so I'm not letting up any. I want to do well so much it makes me sick. . . . I get this nervous stomach, this awful feeling before games, but to me this is a good feeling, because I know I'm ready to play."

It is fortunate that West has remained dedicated to the game. If he hadn't, he might have been retired from the N.B.A. by now. He has been battered and bruised so often on the court that he could easily serve as a walking advertisement for Blue Cross medical insurance. One of the most amazing things about Jerry West is the way he ignores the physical hurts and keeps coming back to play—and plays well.

While playing for West Virginia in a game against Kentucky, he broke his nose for the fourth time in his basketball career. Blood gushed onto the court and West had to be led to the dressing room, where his nose was packed in ice.

"But Jerry wouldn't quit," Schaus has since recalled. "He went out in the second half and scored 19 points, for a 36 total, and we beat Kentucky."

With the Lakers, West has been the same gritty guy. During his rookie year, he drove to the Los Angeles Sports Arena for a game. He didn't expect to play because he was weak from a bad cold. But as soon as he learned that the club's great forward, Elgin Baylor, had the flu and couldn't play, he suited up without a word and stayed on the court for the entire 48 minutes of the game. That night a "weakened" West scored 38 points, had 15 rebounds and led Los Angeles to a 121-116 victory over the Philadelphia Warriors.

The same season, in a game against the Syracuse Nationals, he was knocked down as he drove to the basket, landing heavily on his right hand and his left foot. Laker radio announcer Chick Hearn watched him limp off the court, then told his listeners: "You won't see Jerry West for some time." Less than two minutes later, West was back in the game, darting all over the floor.

West concluded his rookie season by rebounding from still another painful injury. In a play-off game against Detroit, the Pistons' powerful Bob Ferry hit West in the mouth with his elbow so forcefully that he knocked out a tooth. The injury

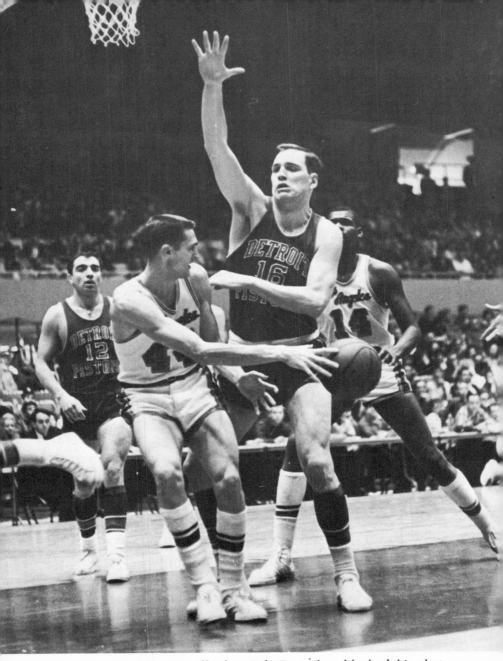

West passes off after Bob Ferry has blocked his shot.

didn't stop Jerry. By the time the play-offs ended, he had scored 275 points in 12 games, achieving a 22.9-points-per-game average—better than his regular season average of 17.6.

In the years that have followed, West has continued to display the kind of toughness and courage that could come only from a man who cares deeply about the game. In the 1962-63 season, he hurtled himself toward the basket on a driving lay-up and slammed into a couple of New York Knicks with such impact that he ripped a hamstring tendon in his leg. This injury was not the most painful in his career, but for West it was the most annoying. With the damaged tendon, he lost his maneuverability on the court and was forced to sit out 25 ball games. When he tried to come back too soon, a habit of his, he reinjured it and had to sit out more games. To no one's surprise, though, he was as good as ever when the time came for the crucial play-off series: in 13 play-off games, West averaged 27.8 points per game.

A year later, West suffered another bad injury when he went scurrying for a loose basketball. In reaching for the ball, he slammed his hand against an opposing player's shin. The player happened to be Wilt Chamberlain, and West came out of the play with a fractured thumb. He missed six games, but had the thumb placed in a cast so he could return to action.

Since then there have been other injuries—a

variety of them, in fact—but in every case West has responded in his tough, proud way. Injuries don't frighten him off. He always comes back strong.

"West gets hurt not because he's frail," said former Laker general manager Lou Mohs, "but because he goes all out and takes chances others won't. . . . And he'll get hurt again, because that's the only way he knows how to play. And we wouldn't have him any other way."

West agrees. "You can't try to protect yourself and still do a job," he says.

As a pro, West goes all out on the court—just as he did years ago in Cheylan. While he was still a rookie in the N.B.A. the report circulated that he didn't dribble well with his left hand. As a result, defenders would guard him a step to his right, forcing him to go left to his weaker shooting side. After his first season, West went to work to correct his flaws. He lined up four or five youngsters at a summer camp he operated, and then tried to maneuver through all of them— dribbling, faking, driving only to his left. Now he can dribble equally well with both hands. But he still wishes he could be a better player. "I practice over and over what I do best," he has said. "I shoot from certain spots, over and over. I practice my moves to get to that spot, over and over."

The constant practice has paid off. Through the years West has had the knack of making a

West dunks the ball in a game against the New York Knickerbockers.

basket when his team most needed it. "Pressure makes me want to play harder," he once said, and his record proves it. He has always played better in games that meant something. In play-offs, for example, he has had a lifetime scoring average of approximately 30 points per game, which is better than his average for regular-season games. In the 11 play-off games he played at the end of the 1964-65 season, he averaged an incredible 40.6 points per game.

"Under emotional stress," Lou Mohs has said, "the average person's bodily functions go out of kilter. Jerry and a few others have themselves under such control that they are not subject to normal human frailties and can operate with complete mechanical perfection. If there is any response to pressure at all, there is a heightening of this mechanical operation, a refining of talent. Jerry is actually better under stress—cooler, more calculating. Everyone wants to be this way, but wanting it isn't enough. It has to be inside of you, and Jerry has it."

This is demonstrated by the fact that West usually guides Los Angeles through the big games. Without him, the Lakers are in trouble. In the 1961-62 season, the Lakers lost their other great star, Elgin Baylor, to the Army for most of the last half of the season, but the team continued to hold first place. The next year they had a 43-12 record until Jerry was sidelined by his hamstring injury. After that they dropped to 10-15, and their first-place lead was cut in half. In the 1963-64 season the Lakers had a 31-19 record until Jerry broke his thumb; then they dropped to 11-19 and were in third place.

Even though West is important to the team, he is not a selfish ballplayer. He knows he must shoot the ball often if the Lakers are to win games, but he is also aware of the rest of the team.

"It's not easy," he has said, "because by nature I don't like to hog the show." One night West had 30 points by half time, and was embarrassed about it. He was afraid his teammates might think he was showing off. "So I stopped shooting," he said. "We won the game, so it was okay. But if we'd lost, maybe it would have been my fault. This is a team game. It's my responsibility to shoot a lot and I'm sure the guys realize it and accept it. Winning any way you can is all that counts."

West is not—and has never been—an easy loser. "I just can't learn to wind down after a losing game," he said. "I can't sleep. It's hard enough at home, but at least I have my family, and I am at home. On the road, it's terrible. I replay the game, try to get rid of it that way, but it doesn't always work. I've taken to reading when I get back to the hotel." But he finds that this doesn't always work either.

Despite emotional and physical problems, West manages to stay at the top of his game. He does it with a blend of natural talent and basket-

West fights the Celtics' Bill Russell for a rebound.

ball know-how. "I am quick," he has said, "which is the one physical thing I have over most players. Straightaway speed doesn't mean much. It's how fast you can move your hands and feet in a limited area of court. I know the defensive players now and, depending on who I'm facing, I vary my moves and shots, the arc and everything, just the way a pitcher changes speeds. I have more percentage shots, the shots I can hit, than most players. . . . All this comes with experience. The action is so fast out there, you can get lost in the shuffle . . . but after a while you get so you can anticipate the way the ball will bounce and can react instantly, instinctively."

In recent years, Jerry's instincts have kept him from injuring himself so much. Of course, he still doesn't shy away from the action. He has simply learned how to cope with the game. "I have a better *feel* of the game," he says. "I have learned how to find the position to make my shot without getting hurt."

But all the instincts in the world do not save West from the battering he must take because of the mad-dash way he plays basketball. Like the little kid in Cheylan, West Virginia, who trudged home with muddy shoes, the grown-up Jerry West can't get enough of the game.

"The way I see it," he once said, "if a man has a job he hates and can't stand going to work every day, then it's about time he started to look for a new job. As for me, I enjoy the game."

10/Oscar Robertson

The best description of Oscar Robertson's basketball philosophy was given by a man who has had to play against Robertson for a living. Dick Barnett, the New York Knicks' fine guard, once said: "Oscar's tough. If you give him a twelve-foot shot, he'll work on you until he's got a ten-foot shot. Give him ten, he wants eight. Give him eight, he wants six. Give him six, he wants four. Give him four, he wants two. Give him two, you know what he wants? That's right, baby. A lay-up."

As Barnett implies, any time the "Big O," as Robertson is called, laces on his sneakers, he's going to try to do a little better than his past performances. "I have the feeling," Oscar's wife, Yvonne, once said, "that he's competing against himself now, even more than against another player or a team. Just to see how much better he can be, how he can do something a little differently and still do it well. Just to keep accomplishing and improving."

Robertson is a basketball perfectionist. This is illustrated by an incident that occurred during a practice session a few seasons ago. Jack McMahon, who was then coaching the Cincinnati Royals, tried to make practice more interesting by holding a foul-shooting contest. McMahon offered a $5 prize for the man who hit the most of 25 free throws. Three Royals promptly made 23 of 25 shots. One of them was Adrian Smith, who had once shot .903 percent from the foul line over the course of a season. But neither Smith nor the other Royals collected McMahon's prize. For Oscar Robertson stepped up to the line and hit 25 consecutive foul shots.

It is not just natural ability that makes the Big O so great. More important is the way he applies it. "Oscar," said Wilt Chamberlain, "is not as fast as some ballplayers or as good a shooter as others, but he knows how to put everything together better than anybody else."

What makes Robertson the best all-round player in the N.B.A.—few people argue this point—is his instinct to be artistically perfect on the court. When he talks about as simple an act as passing the ball he reveals his deep understanding of the game: "All passes aren't good passes just because the ball reaches the teammate you intend it for. If the man has got himself into a good shooting position and your pass pulls him out of it, it's a bad pass. That's what playmaking really is—getting the ball to the man so that he's

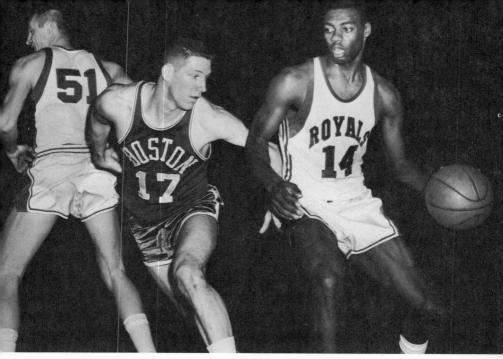

Oscar Robertson drives against Boston's John Havlicek.

in position to take his best shot."

Though Robertson's lifetime statistics are out-standing (he has averaged over 30 points per game and about ten rebounds and ten assists a game), many pros think that he could score more if he wanted to. Oscar's teammate, Jerry Lucas, has said, "If Oscar ever really sets out to see how many points he could score in a single game, there's no telling how high he can go."

But personal glory is not Robertson's big con-cern. He plays to win ball games and, to that end, the 6-foot 5-inch, 218-pound Royal tries to keep his teammates involved in the action. Dick McGuire, ex-New York Knick coach, has said: "I've seen Oscar concentrate on passing. He'll make sure that each of the Royals gets a bucket in the first couple of minutes. Then they're all happy and they play together. Actually, the only time he'll concentrate on scoring is when they're behind."

McGuire might have added that Robertson is a particularly dangerous scorer when he's angry. In fact, N.B.A. coaches have advised their men not to arouse the Big O's temper because it just doesn't pay. During the 1966-67 season a Chicago Bull rookie named Jerry Sloan blocked a shot by Robertson and ended up regretting it. As the Bulls' assistant coach Al Bianchi described the incident, "Suddenly Oscar wasn't dribbling any more. He was pounding the ball into the floor like a pile driver and moving deliberately toward the basket, time after time, pouring through point after point. . . . Now I've got a standing order on my club. When Oscar's mad and starts for the basket, I want the three nearest guys to forget their own men and help out."

Even if his mood is calm Robertson is a big problem to the opposition. When Red Auerbach was coaching the Boston Celtics, there was one season when the Celtics couldn't seem to hold Oscar to fewer than 40 points a game. Auerbach would devise different strategies to limit the Big O's scoring output, but it always ended up the same—Oscar scored his 40 points or more. Finally, Boston "held" Robertson to 37 points and Auerbach jokingly told reporters: "We tried

something new on him. I told the boys to stretch
their fingers out wide, with their hands way up
on defense, figuring every little bit helps. But
you know what Oscar did? He shot through their
fingers."

When Auerbach was coaching, the Celtics
used to rotate three guards against Oscar: the
speedy Sam Jones, defensive specialist K. C.
Jones and rugged John Havlicek. The idea was to
try to wear Robertson down. However, it generally didn't work. Auerbach's successor as
coach, Bill Russell, has abandoned such elaborate
strategy. "I don't think it makes a bit of difference who's covering Oscar," he said. "You just
don't stop him. The way we work it here now, I
let the guards decide that among themselves."
Laughingly he concluded, "The way they've
worked it out is that the one with the worst ex-
cuse gets him."

Robertson may be everybody's idea of the perfect ballplayer now, but there was a time when
basketball wasn't nearly as easy. Oscar grew up
in a ghetto in Indianapolis, Indiana, using a
peach-basket hoop in the back of his family's tar-
paper-roofed house. He and his older brother,
Bailey, used a rag ball held together by an elastic
or, if they were lucky, an old tennis ball found in
a neighborhood alley. But when the opportunity
came to play on real basketball courts, the
younger Oscar wasn't always permitted to play

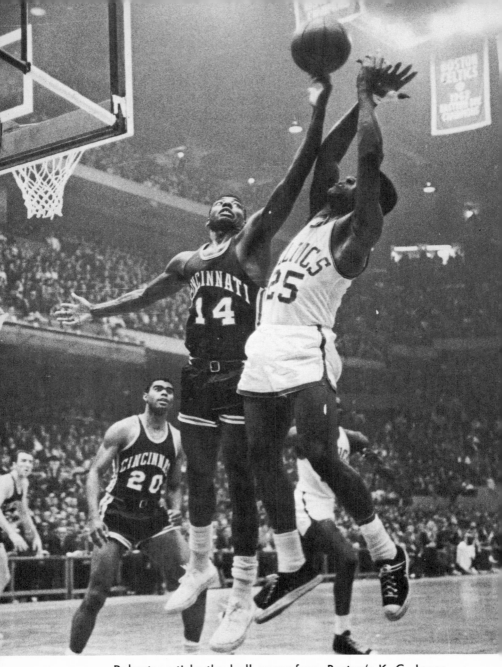

Robertson ticks the ball away from Boston's K. C. Jones.

with the bigger boys. Quite naturally he was angry. "I promised myself," he said, "that I'd get so good that they'd have to let me play. I practiced all the time. I practiced at the Y and at what was called the 'dust bowl,' which was just a little vacant lot a couple of blocks from our house."

Oscar loved the game so much that, wherever he went, he traveled with a basketball. "He was always bouncing it," his mother remembered. "He'd bring it to the dinner table and he took it to bed with him. When the sound of the bumping stopped, we knew that Oscar was ready to go to sleep."

It wasn't long before Robertson was playing with the bigger boys. In fact, he soon was playing better than any of them. While attending Crispus Attucks High School, he led his team to two state titles in a row and 45 consecutive victories. "It was a great thrill," Oscar once said, remembering the first title. "After the game, the local fire department was there with the fire truck, and we all got aboard and rode through town with the siren going, and then we had a bonfire and everything. It was sort of inspiring. It really was."

Robertson played college ball at the University of Cincinnati. When he was a sophomore, he came to the old Madison Square Garden in New York and amazed everybody by scoring 56 points.

During his college career Robertson shot the ball often, but his teammates never begrudged him his scoring. "Oscar made us a team," said teammate Ralph Davis. "He can do anything."

One night, the club was watching Oscar receive a postseason award on television and they heard him say, "It's nice to make All America, but I couldn't have done it without the help of my teammates." At that point a Cincinnati player named Mike Mendenhall jumped up and yelled at the screen, "The devil you couldn't." Later, Mendenhall told a reporter: "He's the greatest. Just the greatest. There isn't a bit of jealousy. I even enjoyed practices. Oscar's that much fun to play with."

However, when Robertson first joined the Cincinnati Royals in 1960, his teammates were not quite as enthusiastic about him. In Robertson's rookie season one sportswriter said that Cincinnati's attack was "as complex as a baby's rattle: Robertson took the ball in bounds, thumped down the floor until he saw a shot or passed off to set up a play."

Robertson's dribbling annoyed his teammates, one of whom said, "I think we've got to run to win. We can't bull our way against these other teams with their big men. We just don't have the big men. If the defenses get set up we have trouble rebounding. If Oscar bounces the ball deliberately, fooling around until he sees an opening or a screen, we can get killed off the boards."

But after a while the Royals stopped complaining about his dribbling and shooting. For, de-

Robertson shoots over Celtic defenders.

spite their initial doubts, they discovered that
when they managed to elude defenders, the Big
O would somehow pass them the ball.

Of course, Oscar didn't stop shooting. In his
rookie season, he averaged 30.5 points per game

and was named to the All-N.B.A. team at the end
of the season—a remarkable feat for a rookie.
Since then, Oscar's seasonal average has never
varied more than two points on either side of 30,
which prompted a long-time basketball expert
to say: "If Oscar walked into your neighborhood
playground for a pickup game, he'd probably
get his 30 and not much more. He's the most con-
sistent star ever."

Robertson is obviously capable of getting more
points, but he is such a brilliant playmaker ("the
only real playmaker to come into the league for
a while," according to Bob Cousy) that he does
not have to score to make Cincinnati's attack effective. By forcing the defense to converge on
him, he can often pass to the Royal who has been
left free for the easy shot.

A good example of Oscar's playmaking knack
is the case of veteran center Connie Dierking. In
his first six seasons in the N.B.A. the 6-foot 10-
inch, 222-pound Dierking had averaged a meager
6.9 points per game. After joining the Royals in
1965, he grew used to working with the Big O,
and learned that if he made precise moves to
shake free of his defender, Robertson would get
the ball to him and he would score more points.
So in the 1967-68 season, Dierking worked hard
to get open and left the rest to Oscar. As a result
he averaged 16.4 points per game—more than he's
averaged during his entire pro career.

Although he is always ready to assist his teammates, Robertson is also quick to scold them for mistakes. According to writer Ed Linn, "As soon as he steps onto the court, the man who has seemed so mild and easygoing begins to crackle with intensity. . . . When anything goes wrong, a look of sheer disbelief comes over Oscar's face. He yells at his teammates, assuming complete command. If the play turns sloppy, both fists shoot into the air and he cries out, 'What's going on here!' "

Ex-Royal coach McMahon has said, "He's the boss man out there. He's giving those guys hell, believe me, and they take it, too. He's a very intense player, burning up inside every minute."

Robertson is also a very sympathetic player. Jackie Moreland, who used to play with the Detroit Pistons, has recalled the time his team lost so many guards because of injuries that he suddenly had to shift from the forward position to a backcourt spot. His defensive assignment was to guard Robertson. "I had a bad leg myself," Moreland said, "and Oscar knew it. But he didn't try to make me look bad. He passed off a lot. I probably couldn't have played him very well on two legs. But the fact that he didn't try to take advantage impressed me more than anything about him."

Robertson didn't try to exploit Moreland's injury because he has no need for cheap baskets. To take advantage of a handicapped player would have proved nothing. For a perfectionist does his best only against the best.

11/Willis Reed

Life for Willis Reed has been a succession of challenges which he has never failed to meet head-on. Even as a boy Willis knew hard times. He had to struggle to help his family survive— and to satisfy his own basic needs. In talking of his childhood, he once said, "I picked cotton when I was nine in order to get me a pair of shoes."

That was in Bernice, Louisiana, a town 10 miles from Hico, where Willis was born. "Moving to Bernice," Reed has since recalled, "was like moving to the big city. Bernice was two red lights long. Hico had no red lights, just a couple of stop signs."

In Bernice, Reed discovered the importance of education. "One summer," he said, "I went into the wheat storehouse and worked just like the grownups. I was a big kid then. Heck, I was in the ninth grade and I was six-five. But the money I made was hard money. I ended up with corns, calluses and blisters on my feet and hands. I

looked at the men around me who had large
families and I said to myself: 'I don't have
enough money to do what I want to do. How can
these people with ten kids take care of themselves
and their families?' I knew then and there I was
going to college."

It seemed to Reed that a basketball scholarship
was his only means of reaching college, so he
began driving himself to become a ballplayer.
Tall for his age, he had an awkwardness that is
common among youths who sprout up all of a
sudden. But Willis wasn't embarrassed by his
clumsiness. He saw it merely as another challenge. On the advice of Lendon Stone, the basketball coach at West Side High in Bernice, he
started to jump rope to improve his coordination.
It worked. Reed became the regular center for
Stone's West Side team.

While he was starring for the local school, he
was also growing. By his sophomore year, he
stood 6 feet 7 inches, a fact that was noted one
day by a man named Fred Hobdy, who was the
basketball coach of Grambling College, an all-
black school in Louisiana.

Hobdy met Reed strictly by chance. While
the coach was waiting for one of his players in a
bus depot, he noticed Willis. "I saw this tall kid
in the street," he said. "I had never seen him
around before. If you're in my business, you make
it a point to get to know a kid that tall, so I walked
up to him and introduced myself. He said he was

only in the tenth grade, but I promised to keep
an eye on him and I told him, even if I never
saw him again, he had a scholarship to Grambling when he graduated."

By the time Willis was ready to graduate,
however, Hobdy had become a frequent visitor
at the Reed home. And he was never reluctant
to describe in detail the wonders of life at Grambling. Hobdy was obviously a good talker, for
Reed went to Grambling.

As it happened, though, football—not basket-
ball—was the big sport at Grambling. The college
had a reputation as a school that produced foot-
ball players good enough for the pros. Coach
Eddie Robinson had sent men like Ernie Ladd,
Buck Buchanan, Willie Davis, Roosevelt Taylor,
Lane Howell, Willie Brown, Nemiah Wilson and
Willie Williams to the American and National
Football leagues straight from Grambling.

When Coach Robinson took a look at Reed,
now grown to a healthy 6 feet 10 inches and a
weight of 235 pounds, he saw the makings of another football star. Hobdy, however, managed
to persuade him to stay away from Willis. "Not
this one, Eddie, please," he said. "This one has
a chance to become a great basketball player."

Reed was not great right away, however. In
fact, he joined the varsity as just an ordinary substitute. A fellow named Tommy Bownes was the
regular center. But Reed worked hard to improve
his weaknesses, which were lack of speed and

jumping ability. Whatever Hobdy prescribed to improve those shortcomings, Reed practiced in earnest. And he never stopped working on his shooting and the moves he used to exploit his great physical strength. Soon Reed was Grambling's starting center.

During his career at Grambling, Reed scored a total of 2,235 points for a 26 points-per-game average. He also led Grambling to three Southwest Athletic Conference championships and the N.A.I.A. title. This established Grambling as the top small-college basketball team in the country. Reed was also named to the Little All-America team three times.

When he was just beginning to feel pleased with his accomplishments, Reed suffered two bitter disappointments. First, he was not selected to play on the U.S. Olympic team that went to Tokyo in 1964. "Actually," said Reed, "I never thought I would make the Olympic squad. We had heard that the team was pretty well picked before the Olympic trials. They were going to take only one guy from the N.A.I.A. and I figured it would be Lucius Jackson." (Jackson played with Pan American College which, as an integrated school, played big-time opponents and received more publicity than all-Negro Grambling.) Still, Reed had hoped that the rumors might prove false and that he would, after all, have a chance to play for his country. When he didn't, he felt snubbed.

He felt even more snubbed when he was not a

number-one draft choice of any N.B.A. team, even though the New York Knickerbockers thought enough of him to select him in the second round.

"How *could* I feel about it?" Reed said later. "I was disappointed. I saw $3,000 [the amount of extra money he figured he could have demanded as a number one choice] flying out the window, but it wasn't only the money. My pride was hurt. I expected to be picked on the first round, which would have meant that somebody considered me the best player in the country. I couldn't blame the Knicks. But I couldn't believe there were that many players in the country better than me."

Reed resolved to meet the challenge of the pro game—and prove he was better than basketball people thought. It took only two days at training camp to convince Coach Eddie Donovan that, even if Willis didn't turn out to be a great player, he certainly was a determined one. The rookie came to Donovan's room one night with a most unusual request.

"Coach," he said, "I'd like to borrow a rule book."

"A rule book?" Donovan asked, scratching his head.

"That's right," Willis replied. "I want to read it."

Donovan was astonished. As he later explained he had "never heard of a player, any player, asking for a rule book before."

Not long afterward, Reed again surprised his coach by his dedication. A week before the regular season was to begin, he twisted his ankle early in an exhibition game against the Boston Celtics. When Donovan ordered Willis to the hospital for immediate x-rays, Reed asked, "Can't I go at half time? I want to sit on the bench and watch Russell's moves." How could any coach object to that kind of enthusiasm?

Once the regular season began, the Knicks found that Reed had more than enthusiasm for the game. He had the facility for scoring points and rebounding at the center position that basketball men admire. "He's the best shooter the Knicks have had since Carl Braun [a set-shooting New York guard from the late 1950s]," said former Knick coach Joe Lapchick. "Reminds me of Pettit," said Red Holzman, the Knick scout who became coach midway through the 1967-68 season. "He conducts himself exactly the same way Bob did when he was a rookie—the way he gets knowledge—the way he takes coaching—the way he picks up things."

Reed's performance on the court brought him more and more praise. In his first meeting with Bill Russell, an old high-school idol, Reed outscored the Celtics' star 20 points to 14 and got only four fewer rebounds. Clearly, he could play against the best centers in the league: Russell, Wilt Chamberlain, Walt Bellamy. In fact, one of

Willis Reed grimaces as he tries to shake the Celtics' Bill Russell and John Thompson.

Reed's problems was the psychological letdown he experienced when playing against the other, less skilled pivotmen in the N.B.A. "I can't figure it out," he said. "Maybe there is an unconscious letdown when I'm not against a Russell or Chamberlain."

A greater problem for Reed was his temper, which resulted from his great enthusiasm and drive. If referees called what Reed considered unjustified fouls against him, he became furious. He sincerely believed that the referees protected the established players and made it harder for rookies.

Harry Gallatin, who had replaced Donovan as Knick coach, tried to convince Willis that his outbursts of temper were futile. "I told him," Gallatin said, "not to argue with the officials. It gets him disturbed and he forgets about basketball. He's got to learn that as a rookie he's not going to get every break his way. Those things happen more for the veterans in our league."

Reed finally stopped worrying about the officials and concentrated solely on basketball. Quietly but quickly, Willis Reed established himself as an N.B.A. star. He scored 1,560 points in his rookie year for a 19.5 points-per-game average and had 1,175 rebounds, breaking the team record of 1,098 held by his own coach, Gallatin. At the end of the season he was named Rookie of the Year.

Reed earned more than honors; he won the re-

spect of his fellow pros as well. The N.B.A. players considered him as tough a player as there
was in the league. "On the offensive boards,"
said Detroit's Dave DeBusschere, "Willis is one
of the toughest men to block out. . . . He's overpowering. Outside of Chamberlain, he is probably the strongest man in the league."

Philadelphia's Chet Walker also had praise for
Reed's power: "He pushes a lot and when he
pushes, people move. He uses his strength very
well." Walker spoke well of Reed's determination,
too. "One of his strong points is that he is aggressive on the offensive boards. He keeps going
up for the ball. I can't keep him off. I have to hold
him with my hands and arms."

In view of all the tribute Reed had earned as a
rookie, it was no wonder he looked forward to
his second year in the league. But shortly after
the start of the 1965-66 season, the Knicks made
a trade for Baltimore center Walt Bellamy. Willis
was no longer a center; instead, he was suddenly
forced to play forward.

Reed found the new challenge a difficult one.
He was used to turning and shooting while facing
the basket, but he was not used to getting himself
open as a forward, to moving without the ball, to
passing from the outside. He also had trouble
playing defense against the quick, smaller for-
wards around the league. Suddenly Reed's scoring and rebounding totals decreased. His inability
to adapt himself to the new position hurt the

Reed guards Wilt Chamberlain.

team. New York lost 15 of its first 21 games, and
Gallatin was replaced by Dick McGuire as
coach.

The change in coaches didn't affect Reed, however. He continued to falter at the forward spot.
To make matters worse, his health was suffering.
He had broken his nose before the season began.
Then he suffered in succession a severely
sprained ankle, a swollen knee, an aching back
and a bone spur on his foot that required surgery
at the end of the season. He was also too heavy
for a forward, having gotten his weight up to
252 pounds for the pivot spot he expected to
play.

"Things got worse and worse," he said, "and
finally my confidence went. In this game, confidence is important. I was praying for the season to be over."

By the time it finally ended, Reed's offensive
figures had dropped considerably from the previous season. He had scored 1,178 points (382
fewer than the year before) for a 15.6 points-
per-game average and had only 883 rebounds.
While the statistics wouldn't have been embar-
rassing for most players, Reed was far from satisfied. He felt that he had not met the challenge.

"Maybe it's good," he said after the season.
"Like in my rookie year when I was hungry and
had to prove myself. It's that all over again. People have said, 'Willis Reed can play center—but
can he play forward?' I've been told that a lot of

Reed contends with Philadelphia's Luke Jackson for a loose ball.

the success of the team will be determined by how I adjust to forward."

Reed adjusted and, thanks to him, the Knicks of 1966-67 made the N.B.A. play-offs for the first time since 1959. Reed had reported to the Knicks at a streamlined 235 pounds and proceeded to play with the fury he had shown as a rookie. In the voting for the January All-Star team, no other forward in the East polled as many votes as Willis. He finished the season by scoring 1,628 points, for

a 20.9 average, and collecting a total of 1,136 rebounds. Although the Knicks lost the play-offs
to Boston in five games, nobody could fault
Reed. He averaged 27.5 during the series. This
time Reed had met the challenge. He could afford
to be proud of himself.

"In this game," he told a sportswriter, "it is
the survival of the fittest. The strong survive—
the weak do not. Now when I play, I look at
those other coaches and I say to myself, 'I told
you so. . . . I showed you.' I'm planning to make
them remember that draft for a long, long time."

12/Dave Bing

In the fall of 1966, Dave Bing was a rookie guard with problems. When he arrived at the Detroit Pistons' training camp in St. Clair, Michigan, veterans Tom Van Arsdale and Eddie Miles were the starting guards and, of course, neither man was willing to let a rookie take his job. Van Arsdale and Miles made that clear quickly. "In the beginning of camp," Bing later recalled, "Chico Vaughn and I would have to go against them [Van Arsdale and Miles]. We were smaller physically. It was depressing for me. They'd try to bully me all over the court."

For the 6-foot 3-inch, 180-pound Bing, that was just one of many problems. What bothered him most were the adjustments he had to make to playing defense among the pros. However, this difficulty didn't seem to surprise the Pistons' player-coach, Dave DeBusschere, who said, "There isn't anybody coming into the N.B.A. who doesn't have a problem with defense."

Bing had come from Syracuse University, where he had been an All America, accustomed to a pressing, gambling defense. In college he had always looked for an opportunity to steal the ball from the dribbler. So he'd try to anticipate a player's moves and sometimes he'd ignore his own defensive assignment to double-team another opponent.

It was a defense that worked well for Syracuse, but not for the pros. "Once the ball was passed over him," said Donnis Butcher, an assistant to DeBusschere, "he'd turn his head and chase it. Naturally, that'd leave his man open."

Bing had to learn that to leave a shooter open is to invite disaster, because the pros shoot the ball so well.

In addition to Bing's defensive problems, there were certain pressures on him that made life even harder. They stemmed from the fact that Detroit basketball fans had not wanted Bing when he was drafted at the end of the 1965-66 season. The city had wanted Cazzie Russell. Russell had played at the University of Michigan, where he had been the outstanding college player in the country. Twice during his college career, his presence had sold out Detroit's Cobo Arena, something the losing Pistons could never do. With Russell on the team, the fans thought, the Pistons would become a winner.

That year Detroit had finished last in the Western Division. The New York Knicks had finished

Dave Bing of Syracuse University intimidates a shooter.

last in the Eastern Division. A flip of the coin was to determine which of the two teams got first choice in the draft of college players, which meant getting Cazzie Russell. At the coin-tossing ceremony the Pistons called "tails," and the next day the headlines in the Detroit *Free Press* said: "SAD 'TAIL'—PISTONS LOSE FLIP FOR CAZZIE."

The Knicks took Russell and Bing became the Pistons' choice, though not necessarily the choice of Detroit fans. As a result, Bing knew he had to prove himself.

But Dave Bing was used to not being accepted right away. He could remember that, as a boy growing up in the northeast section of Washington, D.C., he had not been able to get a chance to play basketball at the Kelly Miller playground. When he became older, he had gotten his opportunity to compete and had made the best of it.

In Detroit, he was determined to do it again. At training camp, he started to adapt himself to the N.B.A. style of basketball and his defense improved. He also began to fit in with the Pistons' offensive patterns.

Unfortunately, Bing did not make a particularly exciting debut in his first professional game, which was played against the Cincinnati Royals. He did not start, and when he did get into the game he was nervous. "I thought I might start," he has said. "When I didn't, I was psychologically torn up."

Bing drives past Gary Gray (15) and Connie Dierking (24) of the Royals.

Bing played 16 minutes, took six shots and did not make any of them. "It was the only time in my life I've gone scoreless," he said. "I was really depressed. I could hear remarks the people in the stands were making. . . . I knew I'd looked like a flop."

Bing shrugged off his bad start and simply worked harder. Slowly, he gained confidence. He was still not a starter, but whenever he got into a game he scored points. Throughout the first third of the season, he kept coming off the bench to score, each time learning more and more.

In Detroit's first game with Boston, Celtic coach Bill Russell assigned K. C. Jones to guard Bing when he came into the game. The night before, Bing had scored 18 points as a part-timer and Russell didn't want him to do that against the Celtics. Jones, known as the league's toughest defensive guard, made sure Bing didn't score—at least for the first half—and at half time, Bing had no points. But in the last half it was a different story, and Jones came away impressed with the rookie.

"Dave is a real cool one," K.C. said at the end of the game. "I gave him very few chances to shoot during the first half. But instead of just standing around, the way most rookies would, he helped out in other ways. Dave moved the ball well. He passed to the open man and played good defense. And he got away from me enough in the second half to score in double figures. Not many rookies come into this league and take charge the way Bing has."

Pretty soon, Bing was playing well enough to merit a chance as a starter. As he once had on the Kelly Miller playground, Dave took advantage of his opportunity. In his first start against New York, he scored 20 points. His next game was against Los Angeles and that night Bing did everything—scoring, rebounding and setting up plays. On two occasions he grabbed rebounds and, while still in the air, flipped the ball into the basket, despite being surrounded by taller players. Once he switched hands in midair and dropped in a short left-handed jumper. He wound up that evening with a total of 35 points.

By the end of the season, Bing's scoring was even more impressive. On the night that Butcher replaced DeBusschere as Detroit coach, Bing hit his season's high of 47 points against the Baltimore Bullets. That total was only five points short of the club record of 52 points set by George Yardley in the 1957-58 season.

Bing experienced a particularly satisfying game when Detroit played the Philadelphia 76ers at Syracuse, the city where Dave had played his college basketball. That night he scored 20 points and a standing-room crowd of more than 8,000 persons cheered every move he made. Afterward, Bing said with a smile: "I guess I've made it. They want me to come here and give a speech after the season in support of

Syracuse's building program."

Indeed, Bing had made it, and not just in Syracuse. Even Detroit fans were rooting for him. "Once Dave became a starter," said George Maskin, the Pistons' publicity director, "our gate began to jump. We had 120,000 customers the year before. This year with Dave we've had 200-000. Immediately after he became a starter the crowds got bigger. We had four 10,000 crowds, which was unprecedented in our history."

Detroit fans were paying to see Bing's midair magic. Not since Elgin Baylor had come into the league had a ballplayer moved through the air with such facility. Though Bing was only 6 feet 3 inches tall, relatively small for a basketball player, he jumped like a man inches taller. When he set off on a long striding drive the common lay-up shot became an acrobatic adventure. The wiry Piston could stay in the air longer than the average player, an ability that enabled him to switch the ball from one hand to the other to get by soaring foes and score.

In his first year as a pro, Bing led Detroit in scoring with 20 points per game (10th in the N.B.A.) and assists with 4.1 a game (11th in the N.B.A.). He also grabbed an average of 4.4 rebounds a game. His presence in the line-up roused the Pistons. The season before Bing came to Detroit, the Pistons had a 22-58 record, the worst in their history. After Bing joined the team, they improved their game considerably. But un-

Bing demonstrates some of his midair magic.

fortunately not even Dave could prevent them from finishing in last place. Despite that, Bing was voted Rookie of the Year.

But the young guard still had his problems. Although Bing had sharpened his defense, Coach Butcher felt that there was room for improvement. He also wanted Bing to help the Pistons more with his scoring. So the coach sat down and had a talk with his star. "I told him," said Butcher, "that I wanted him to shoot the ball more. He's so modest that I was afraid maybe he felt he shouldn't have more shots."

With that in mind, Bing began to prepare himself for his second season in professional basketball. During the summer, he would go from his job at a Detroit bank straight to an outdoor basketball court, where teammate Eddie Miles would be waiting for him. "We played a lot during the summer," Dave said. "People think of Miles as just a shooter, but he showed me a lot defensively."

Miles also helped him offensively. "We played a lot of one-on-one," Bing said. "Eddie is physically strong. He beats you bodily. A lot of times I'd get by him, but he'd nudge me just a little with his hip or arm. He was getting me used to being hit on the drives."

The practice paid large dividends, for in the 1967-68 season Bing found himself making the driving shots he'd missed the year before when he'd been bumped by defensive men. In fact, he was making considerably more shots of all sorts. Suddenly he was no longer the tenth best scorer in the N.B.A. but the league's leader—he scored 2,142 points, more than any other player.

His defense was better, too. For example, against Seattle one night Bing stole the ball from the Supersonics' rookie center, Bob Rule, with 18 seconds remaining in the game. The steal, one of several he made that night, preserved the Pistons' slim two-point lead and helped secure a victory.

With his quick reflexes and determination, Bing also was learning to stick close to his man. He had rid himself of the bad habit of turning when the ball was passed over his head. Now he focused his attention on the man he was assigned to guard. And though Butcher said, "He still has a tendency to anticipate what his man's going to do—rather than just playing the man," it was apparent the coach was pleased with Dave's improvement.

Bing also convinced his opponents that he could not be bullied on the court, despite his slender build. "A lot of people thought I'd have a tough time because I was skinny," Bing said, "but I didn't. I think this weight thing is overemphasized. You can be small and still be strong."

Other pros agreed that Bing didn't have to worry about being roughed up. "He's skinny, but nobody pushes him around," said Flynn Robinson of Chicago. "That's because he's tough."

Bing scores against the St. Louis Hawks.

Even Bing's playmaking improved in his sophomore season. As a rookie he had upset the Pistons by throwing flashy passes while in midair. In his second year, however, his teammates were ready for him. As a result, Bing rose from 11th place in assists to become one of the league's leaders.

Although DeBusschere, Miles and "Happy" Hairston also sparked the team in the 1967-68 season, Bing was the player who made the Pistons a force to be reckoned with on the court. And for the first time since the 1962-63 season they earned a place in the play-offs.

It is interesting to note that before Dave came to Detroit, the hottest item on basketball nights was a local character named Gus, who would stand in the balcony and, to the accompaniment of the house organ, dance the "frug" during time-outs. These days Gus still dances in the aisles, but he's just a sideshow now. Dave Bing has made the Pistons the number-one attraction in town.

Index

About the Author

Phil Berger, formerly an editor with *Sport* Magazine, is a freelance writer who lives in New York City. He contributes regularly to *Sport, Dare* and *The National Observer.* He is also the author of *Championship Teams of the N.F.L.* (Punt, Pass & Kick Library #10).